Pets Welcome!
California

P9-DUB-453

As "cover girl," officer manager of Bon Vivant Press

and owner of authors, Robert and Kathleen Fish,

I would like to share the joys of our vacations and working

trips to produce our *Cooking Secrets* series. Special thanks

to my bon vivant canine pals, Page, Rugen, Rocky and Joey.

— *Dreamer Dawg*

CALIFORNIA EDITION

Pets Welcome

A Guide to Hotels, Inns, and Resorts That Welcome You and Your Pet

KATHLEEN AND ROBERT FISH

BON VIVANT

Library of Congress Cataloging-in-Publication Data
Pets Welcome™ California:
A Guide to Hotels, Inns and Resorts That Welcome You and Your Pet
Fish, Kathleen DeVanna
97-071559
ISBN 1-883214-12-2
$15.95 softcover
Includes indexes

Copyright ©1997 by Kathleen DeVanna Fish
Cover photography by Robert N. Fish
Editorial direction by Charlotte D. Atkins
Editorial assistance by Susan Parkes
Cover design by Morris Design
Illustrations by Krishna Gopa, Graphic Design & Illustration and
Gerrica Connolly, Design Studio
Type by Cimarron Design

Published by Bon Vivant Press
a division of The Millennium Publishing Group
P.O. Box 1994
Monterey, CA 93942

Printed in the United States of America
by Publishers Press

Contents

Introduction

Traveling with people we love and whose company we enjoy can be one of life's great pleasures. Our pets can be counted among those who enrich our lives. So it is little wonder that over 40 million of us choose to take our pets along with us when we travel.

Whether embarking on a wine-tasting adventure in Northern California's Napa Valley or Sonoma regions, exploring the breathtaking Central Coast's natural bounty that has awed and inspired artists and romantics for decades or setting out on a sightseeing safari to the San Diego Zoo or other Southern California attractions, we offer you recommendations for unforgettable places to stay.

The wonderful thing is that hundreds of hotels, inns, guest ranches and bed and breakfasts throughout California welcome pets with open arms.

Of course, just as they each offer different amenities and accommodations, they also have a wide range of pet policies.

That's why Pets Welcome™ will be a handy resource for you, to help you discover and select some of the best places to stay when traveling with your four-legged companions. We have researched and ranked a broad spectrum of places, from romantic hideaways to inns that have made a trademark name for themselves in the hospitality industry.

For example, when planning a day in Napa Valley exploring and sampling the vineyards' best, you might want to start at Calistoga, famous for its hot springs and local charm, too. There you will find the enchanting cottages of the Washington Street Lodging within walking distance of downtown Calistoga. When venturing into quaint Carmel-by-the-Sea, local inns such as the Cypress Inn offer you a touch of history, an abundance of style and unparalleled scenic splendor in one of California's most pet-friendly environments. A single visit to Carmel Beach reveals the lofty place dogs hold in the community.

Of course, some find comfort in name recognition and industry names such as Residence Inn by Marriott tell travelers they are ensured of home-style accommodations. And it wouldn't seem like home without your pet, now would it?

Each hotel or inn was chosen because of its ambiance, special charm, guest amenities and, of course, its pet friendliness. We have bestowed each with our three-, four- or five-paw designation.

In addition, original pen-and-ink artist renderings share a glimpse of each place's awaiting character and charm.

We have included lodging that should meet all types of travel needs and budgets, from luxurious and romantic or high-tech and convenient to secluded and quirky or warm and rustic.

In addition to the accommodation summaries, this guide book provides maps and details on points of interest throughout California, including parks, beaches and wineries.

Whether you and your pet are travel veterans or setting out on a trip together for the first time, you'll no doubt learn a valuable lesson or two from the travel tips provided by the Humane Society of the United States. These helpful hints offer insight into traveling by car, plane and other modes of transportation, offering specialized guidance on crating animals, documentation and basic care and courtesy information. Being an informed pet owner will make your trip more enjoyable and comfortable for both you and your animal.

It is our hope that as you travel throughout California, you will return time and time again to this book as you would to your favorite inn—finding comfort in knowing that the places found within welcome both you and your pet, that details are both useful and intriguing and that it can open doors to new and exciting adventures. In fact, we hope you use it so much that it becomes, well, dog-eared.

Abbreviations Used in this Book

AAA	American Automobile Association
ABA	American Breeders Association
AKC	American Kennel Club
AARP	American Association of Retired Persons

Top Ten Travel Tips

1 Bring your pet's own food, dishes, litter and litter box, leash, collar with ID tags, a first aid kit and a bottle of water from home. This will make your pet more comfortable, prepare you for emergencies and decrease the chances of an upset stomach from a strange brand of food. Maintain the normal feeding and walking schedule as much as possible. Be sure to bring old bath towels or paper towels in case of an accident and plastic bags to dispose of your pet's waste. It is a good idea to bring a picture of your pet for identification purposes in case you and your pet become separated.

2 Bring your pet's vaccination records with you when traveling in state, and a health certificate when traveling out of state. If you plan on boarding him at anytime during your vacation, call the boarding kennel to reserve his space, see what they require you to bring and if they require a health certificate.

3 Bring your pet's favorite toys, leash, grooming supplies, medications and bedding. It is a good idea to bring an old sheet or blanket from home to place over the hotel's bedding, just in case your pet gets on the bed. It will also come in handy to protect your car seats from hair and dirty paws.

4 Tape the address of where you are staying on the back of your pet's ID tag or add a laminated card or new ID tag to your pet's collar, or add a second collar with a friend or family members phone number. This information is also good to have on your pet's collar in case of a natural disaster so that someone out of your area can be contacted if you and your pet become separated.

5 Do not leave your pets unattended in a hotel room. The surroundings are new and unfamiliar to your animal and may cause him to become upset and destroy property he normally would not or bark excessively and disturb your neighbors. You also run the risk of his escaping. If a maid should open the door to clean your room, the pet may see this as a chance to find you and escape, or worse, he may attack the maid out of fear.

6 Train your pet to use a crate. This will come in handy if you ever need to travel by plane. Make sure the crate has enough room for your pet to stand up comfortably and turn around inside. Be sure to trim your pet's nails so that they don't get caught in the crate door or ventilation holes. Crates come in handy in hotel rooms, too. If your pet is already used to being in a crate, he will not object if you leave him in one long enough for you to go out to breakfast. Never take your pet with you if you will have to leave him in the car. If it is 85 degrees outside, within minutes the inside of the car can reach over 160 degrees, even with the windows cracked, causing heat stroke and possible death. According to The Humane Society of the United States, the signs of heat stress are: heavy panting, glazed eyes, a rapid pulse, unsteadiness, a staggering gait, vomiting, or a deep red or purple tongue. If heat stroke does occur, the pet must be cooled by dousing him with water and applying ice packs to his head and neck. He should then be taken to a veterinarian immediately.

7 When your pet is confined to a crate, the best way to provide water for your pet is to freeze water in the cup that hooks onto the door of your pet's crate. This way they will get needed moisture without the water splashing all over the crate. Freezing water in your pet's regular water bowl also works well for car trips.

8 Be sure to put your pet's favorite toys and bedding in the crate. Label the crate with "LIVE ANIMAL" and "THIS END UP," plus the address and phone number of your destination, as well as your home address and phone number and the number of someone to contact in case of an emergency.

9 When traveling by plane, be sure to book the most direct flights possible. The less your pet has to be transferred from plane to plane, the less chance of your being separated. This is also important when traveling in hot or cold weather. You don't want your pet to have to wait in the cargo hold of a plane or be exposed to bad weather for any longer than necessary. Check with airlines for the type of crate they require and any additional requirements. They are very strict about the size and type of crate you may carry on board.

10 Do not feed your pet before traveling. This reduces the risk of an upset stomach or an accident in his crate or your car. When traveling by car, remember that your pet needs rest stops as often as you do. It is a good idea for everyone to stretch their legs from time to time. If your pet is unfamiliar with car travel, then get him use to the car gradually. Start a few weeks before your trip with short trips around town and extend the trips a little each time. Then he will become accustomed to the car before your trip and it will be more pleasant for all involved.

Traveling With Your Pet

Courtesy of The Humane Society of the United States (HSUS)
2100 "L" Street, N.W.
Washington, D.C. 20037
© 1995 HSUS. All rights reserved.

If you are planning a trip and you share your life with a pet, you have a few decisions to make before you set off. The following are tips to help you plan a safer and smoother trip for both you and your pet.

SHOULD YOU TRAVEL WITH YOUR PET?

Some pets are not suited for travel because of temperament, illness or physical impairment. If you have any doubts about whether it is appropriate for your pet to travel, talk to your veterinarian.

If you decide that your pet should not travel with you, consider the alternatives: Have a responsible friend or relative look after your pet, board your pet at a kennel or hire a sitter to visit, feed and exercise your pet.

If a friend or relative is going to take care of your pet, ask if that person can take your pet into his or her home. Animals can get lonely when left at home alone. Be sure your pet is comfortable with his or her temporary caretaker and any pets that person has.

If you choose to board your pet, get references and inspect the kennel. Your veterinarian or local shelter can help you select a facility. If you are hiring a sitter, interview the candidates and check their references. (A pet sitter may be preferable if your pet is timid or elderly and needs the comfort of familiar surroundings during your absence.)

Whatever option you choose, there are a few things to remember. Your pet should be up-to-date on all vaccinations and in sound health. Whoever is caring for your pet should know the telephone number at which you can be reached, the name and telephone number of your veterinarian and your pet's medical or dietary needs. Be sure your pet is comfortable with the person you have chosen to take care of him or her.

If You Plan to Travel with Your Pet

THE PRE-TRIP VETERINARY EXAMINATION

Before any trip, have your veterinarian examine your pet to ensure that he or she is in good health. A veterinary examination is a requisite for obtaining legal documents required for many forms of travel.

In addition to the examination, your veterinarian should provide necessary vaccinations such as rabies, distemper, infectious hepatitis and leptospirosis. If your pet is already up-to-date on these, obtain written proof.

Your veterinarian may prescribe a tranquilizer for the pet who is a nervous traveler; however, such drugs should be considered only after discussion with your veterinarian. He or she may recommend a trial run in which your pet is given the prescribed dosage so you can observe the effects. Do not give your pet any drug not prescribed or given to you by your veterinarian.

LEGAL REQUIREMENTS

When traveling with your pet, it is always advisable to keep a health certificate (a document from your veterinarian certifying that your pet is in good health) and medical records close at hand. If you and your pet will be traveling across state lines, you must obtain from your veterinarian a certificate of rabies vaccination.

Although pets may travel freely throughout the United States as long as they have proper documentation, Hawaii requires a 120-day quarantine for all dogs and cats. Hawaii's quarantine regulations vary by species, so check prior to travel.

If you and your pet are traveling from the United States to Canada, you must carry a certificate issued by a veterinarian that clearly identifies the animal and certifies that the dog or cat has been vaccinated against rabies during the preceding 36-month period. Different Canadian provinces may have different requirements. Be sure to contact the government of the province you plan to visit.

If you and your pet are traveling to Mexico, you must carry a health certificate prepared by your veterinarian within two weeks of the day you cross the border. The certificate must include a description of your pet, the lot number of the rabies vaccine used, indication of distemper vaccination and a veterinarian's statement that the animal is free from infectious or contagious disease. This certificate must be stamped by an office of the U.S. Department of Agriculture (USDA). The fee for the stamp is $4.

Get Ready to Hit the Road

TRAVEL CARRIERS

Travel carriers are useful when your pet is traveling by car; they are mandatory when your pet is traveling by air. Your pet's carrier should be durable and smooth-edged with opaque sides, a grille door and several ventilation holes on each of the four sides. Choose a carrier with a secure door and latch. If you are traveling by air, the carrier should have food and water dishes. Pet carriers may be purchased from pet-supply stores or bought directly from domestic airlines. Select a carrier that has enough room to permit your animal to sit and lie down but is not large enough to allow your pet to be tossed about during travel. You can make the carrier more comfortable by lining the interior with shredded newspaper or a towel. (For air-travel requirements, see the "Traveling by Air" section.)

It is wise to acclimate your pet to the carrier in the months or weeks preceding your trip. Permit your pet to explore the carrier. Place your pet's food dish inside the carrier and confine him or her to the carrier for brief periods.

To introduce your pet to car travel in the carrier, confine him or her in the carrier and take short drives around the neighborhood. If properly introduced to car travel, most dogs and cats will quickly adjust to and even enjoy car trips.

CAREFUL PREPARATION IS KEY

When packing, don't forget your pet's food, food and water dishes, bedding, litter and litter box, leash, collar and tags, grooming supplies and a first aid kit and any necessary medications. Always have a container of drinking water with you.

Your pet should wear a sturdy collar with ID tags throughout the trip. The tags should have both your permanent address and telephone number and an address and telephone number where you or a contact can be reached during your travels.

Traveling can be upsetting to your pet's stomach. Take along ice cubes, which are easier on your pet than large amounts of water. You should keep feeding to a minimum during travel. (Provide a light meal for your pet two or three hours before you leave if you are traveling by car and four to six hours before departure if you are traveling by airplane.) Allow small amounts of water periodically in the hours before the trip.

On Your Way

TRAVELING BY CAR

Dogs who enjoy car travel need not be confined to a carrier if your car has a restraining harness (available at pet-supply stores) or if you are accompanied by a passenger who can restrain the dog. Because most cats are not as comfortable traveling in cars, for their own safety as well as yours, it is best to keep them in a carrier.

Dogs and cats should always be kept safely inside the car. Pets who are allowed to stick their heads out the window can be injured by particles of debris or become ill from having cold air forced into their lungs. Never transport a pet in the back of an open pickup truck.

Stop frequently to allow your pet to exercise and eliminate. Never permit your pet to leave the car without a collar, ID tag and leash.

Never leave your pet unattended in a parked car. On warm days, the temperature in your car can rise to 160 degrees in a matter of minutes, even with the windows opened slightly. Furthermore, an animal left alone in a car is an invitation to pet thieves.

TRAVELING BY AIR

Although thousands of pets fly every year without experiencing problems, there are still risks involved. The Humane Society recommends that you do not transport your pet by air unless absolutely necessary.

If you must transport your companion animal by air, call the airline to check health and immunization requirements for your pet.

If your pet is a cat or a small dog, take him or her on board with you. Be sure to contact airlines to find out the specific requirements for this option. If you pursue this option, you have two choices: Airlines will accept either hard-sided carriers or soft-sided carriers, which may be more comfortable for your pet. Only certain brands of soft sided carriers are acceptable to certain airlines, so call your airline to find out what carrier to use.

If your pet must travel in the cargo hole, you can increase the chances of a safe flight for your pet by following these tips:

- Use direct flights. You will avoid the mistakes that occur during airline transfers and possible delays in getting your pet off of the plane.

- Always travel on the same flight as your pet. Ask the airline if you can watch your pet being loaded and unloaded into the cargo hold.

- When you board the plane, notify the captain and at least one flight attendant that your pet is traveling in the cargo hold. If the captain knows that pets are on board, he or she may take special precautions.

- Do not ship pug-nosed dogs and cats such as Pekinese, Chow Chows and Persians in the cargo hold. These breeds have short nasal passages that leave them vulnerable to oxygen deprivation and heat stroke in cargo holds.

- If traveling during the summer or winter months, choose flights that will accommodate temperature extremes. Early morning or late evening flights are better in the summer; afternoon flights are better in the winter.

- Fit your pet with two pieces of identification—a permanent ID tag with your name and home address and telephone number and a temporary travel ID with the address and telephone number where you or a contact person can be reached.

- Affix a travel label to the carrier, stating your name, permanent address and telephone number and final destination. The label should clearly state where you or a contact person may be reached as soon as the flight arrives.

- Make sure your pet's nails have been clipped to protect against their hooking in the carrier's door, holes and other crevices.

- Give your pet at least a month before your flight to become familiar with the travel carrier. This will minimize his or her stress during travel.

- Your pet should not be given tranquilizers unless they are prescribed by your veterinarian. Make sure your veterinarian understands that this prescription is for air travel.

- Do not feed your pet for four to six hours prior to air travel. Small amounts of water can be given before the trip. If possible, put ice cubes in the water tray attached to the inside of your pet's kennel. A full water bowl will only spill and cause discomfort.

- Try not to fly with your pet during busy travel times such as holidays and summer. Your pet is more likely to undergo rough handling during hectic travel periods.

- Carry a current photo of your pet with you. If your pet is lost during the trip, a photograph will make it easier for airline employees to search effectively.

- When you arrive at your destination, open the carrier as soon as you are in a safe place and examine your pet. If anything seems wrong, take your pet to a veterinarian immediately. Get the results of the examination in writing, including the date and time.

Do not hesitate to complain if you witness the mishandling of an animal—either yours or someone else's—at any airport.

If you have a bad experience when shipping your animal by air, contact The HSUS, the U.S. Department of Agriculture (USDA) and the airline involved. To contact the USDA write to: USDA, Animal, Plant and Health Inspection Service (APHIS), Washington, D.C. 20250.

TRAVELING BY SHIP

With the exception of assistance dogs, only a few cruise lines accept pets—normally only on ocean crossings and frequently confined to kennels. Some lines permit pets in private cabins. Contact cruise lines in advance to find out their policies and which of their ships have kennel facilities. If you must use the ship's kennel, make sure it is protected from the elements.

Follow the general guidelines suggested for other modes of travel when planning a ship voyage.

TRAVELING BY TRAIN

Amtrak currently does not accept pets for transport unless they are assistance dogs. (There may be smaller U.S. railroad companies that permit animals on board their trains.) Many trains in European countries allow pets. Generally, it is the passengers' responsibility to feed and exercise their pets at station stops.

HOTEL ACCOMMODATIONS

There are approximately 8,000 hotel, motels and inns across the United States that accept guests with pets. Most hotels set their own policies, so it is important to call ahead and ask if pets are permitted and if there is a size limit.

IF YOUR PET IS LOST

Whenever you travel with your pet, there is a chance that you and your pet will become separated. It only takes a moment for an animal to stray and become lost. If your pet is missing, immediately canvas the area. Should your pet not be located within a few hours, take the following action:

- Contact the animal control departments and humane societies within a 60-mile radius of where your pet strayed. Check with them each day.

- Post signs at intersections and in store fronts throughout the area.

- Provide a description and a photograph of your missing pet to the police, letter carriers or delivery people.

- Advertise in newspapers and with radio stations. Be certain to list your hotel telephone number on all lost-pet advertisements.

A lost pet may become confused and wary of strangers. Therefore, it may be days, or even weeks, before the animal is retrieved by a Good Samaritan. If you must continue on your trip or return home, arrange for a hotel clerk or shelter employee to contact you if your pet is located.

DO YOUR PART TO MAKE PETS WELCOME GUESTS

Many hotels, restaurants and individuals will give your pet special consideration during your travels. It is important for you to do your part to ensure that dogs and cats will continue to be welcomed as traveling companions. Obey local animal-control ordinances, keep your animal under restraint and be thoughtful and courteous to other travelers.

If you have more specific questions or are traveling with a companion animal other than a dog or cat, contact the Companion Animals section of the HSUS.

HELPFUL HINTS

- To transport birds out of the United States, record the leg-band or tattoo number on the USDA certificate and get required permits from the U.S Fish and Wildlife Service.

- Carry a current photograph of your pet with you. If your pet is lost during a trip, a photograph will make it easier for others (airline employees, the police, shelter workers, etc.) to help find your pet.

- While thousands of pets fly without problems every year, there are risks involved. The HSUS recommends that you do not transport your pet by air unless absolutely necessary.

- Whenever you travel with your pet, there is a chance that you and your pet will be separated. If your pet is lost, immediately canvas the area and take appropriate action.

Shasta Lake

NEVADA

Mendocino

South Lake Tahoe

Sonoma • Napa • SACRAMENTO

Mono Lake

SAN FRANCISCO • Berkeley

Yosemite National Park

• Palo Alto

San Jose •

Santa Cruz •

Monterey •

Carmel •

Big Sur •

Fresno

Death Valley
National Monument

San Simeon •

San Luis Obispo •

Santa Barbara •

Ventura •   Simi Valley

Santa Monica •

LOS ANGELES •   Anaheim

Long Beach •

Palm Springs

San Diego •

Northern California

Antioch
Ramada Inn...21

Arcata
Quality Inn – Mad River...22

Blairsden
Feather River Park Resort...23

Bodega Bay
Bodega Coast Inn...24

Bolinas
Elfriede's Beach Haus...25

Booneville
*Anderson Creek Inn
Bed and Breakfast...26*

Burlingame
Airport Doubletree Hotel...27

Calistoga
The Pink Mansion...28
Triple-S-Ranch...29
Washington Street Lodging...30

Cameron Park
Cameron Park Inn...31

Carnelian Bay
Lakeside Chalets...32

Chico
Holiday Inn...33

Colma
*Golden Lotus Bed and Breakfast
Inn...34*

Concord
*Sheraton Hotel and
Conference Center...35*

Elk
Greenwood Pier Inn...36

Eureka
The Eureka Inn...37

Fortuna
Country Inn – Best Western...38

Fremont
Residence Inn by Marriott...39

Geyserville
Isis Oasis Lodge...40

Glen Ellen
The Big Dog Inn...41

Graeagle
Gray Eagle Lodge...42

Headlsburg
Madrona Manor...43

Hope Valley
Sorensen's Resort...44

Ramada Inn

Ramada Inn
2436 Mahogany Way
Antioch, CA 94509
800-228-2828
(510) 754-6600

Room Rates:	$57–$92, continental breakfast included, AAA and AARP discounts.
Pet Charges or Deposits:	$10 plus $25 cleaning fee and $100 deposit.
Rated: 3 Paws 🐾🐾🐾	117 rooms and suites with refrigerators, some microwaves, in-room safes, laundry and dry cleaning service and conference facilities.

T he heart of the scenic "California Delta" is home to the Antioch – Ramada Inn. The inn offers numerous amenities, spacious rooms and suites and easy access to the wine country, the Sacramento River and the San Joaquin River.

The delta area is abundant with natural beauty, winding waterways, parks and aquatic playgrounds. Here you can go boating, fishing or participate in various water sports. If you prefer, relax by the outdoor heated pool and soak up some sun. The spacious grounds of the inn and nearby park are scenic places for you and your dog to get some exercise. Or pack a picnic lunch and head down to the waterfront for the day.

Quality Inn – Mad River

Quality Inn – Mad River
3535 Janes Road
Arcata, CA 95521
800-221-2222
(707) 822-0409

Room Rates:	$49–$112, AAA and AARP discounts.
Pet Charges or Deposits:	$5 per day; one pet per room.
Rated: 3 Paws 🐾🐾🐾	65 rooms and suites, conference facilities, pool, whirlpool, tennis court, exercise room, playground, sports court, game room, restaurant and cocktail lounge.

T ucked in the heart of redwood country on 12 acres, the Quality Inn – Mad River offers guests comfortable and affordable lodging in a country setting. Families will appreciate the playground and game room to entertain youngsters while parents relax by the pool, play tennis, soak in the hot tub or work out in the exercise facilities.

The inn's restaurant and lounge, the Mad River Saloon and Eatery, is fun for the entire family. Your dog will enjoy the landscaped grounds and exercise area or a chance to explore the nearby rivers and redwood forest. Dog daycare is available upon request.

Feather River Park Resort

Feather River Park Resort
Blairsden, CA 96103
(916) 836-2328

Room Rates: $82–$182, no credit cards accepted.
Rated: 3 Paws 🐾🐾🐾   Housekeeping cabins with private bath, kitchen, fireplace,
                               barbecue, laundry facilities, pools, recreational facility,
                               playground, golf and tennis.

Feather River Park Resort is situated on 160 acres of the Mohawk Valley in Plumas County in the heart of the High Sierras "Lake Country." This old-fashioned haven offers guests and their families, including your pets, meadows, vast canyons, crystal clear streams and lakes, with lots of country-side to explore.

Your log cabin, built in the early 1900s, offers such creature comforts as a fully equipped kitchen, private bath, fireplace and barbecue. Everything is supplied for you, even your linens and bedding.

Activities include swimming, bicycling, volleyball, ping pong, golf, tennis and a playground for the kids. For real outdoor adventures, there are hiking trails, horseback riding and the best trout fishing you could ask for within minutes of the resort.

Bodega Coast Inn

Bodega Coast Inn
521 Coast Highway 1
Bodega Bay, CA 94923
800-346-6999
(707) 875-2217

Room Rates: $79–$199, AAA and AARP discounts.
Pet Charges or Deposits: $15 per night
Rated: 3 Paws 🐾🐾🐾   44 rooms with views, fireplaces and refrigerators. Garden
                         courtyard with spa facing the bay.

Perched a mere 50 yards from the water's edge, The Bodega Coast Inn is at Bodega Bay on the Sonoma Coast north of the Point Reyes Peninsula. Nearby Bodega Head offers hiking trails and an ideal spot to watch the annual whale migrations. "One of 10 most beautiful golf courses in Northern California" is a mere half-mile south of the inn.

Bird watchers flock to the area to view the nearly 200 species of birds that frequent the bay's shores, hence the impetus for Alfred Hitchcock's locally filmed thriller "The Birds."

Each room sports a balcony and view facing the ocean or harbor. A garden terrace spa with bay views is the place to relax at the end of the day.

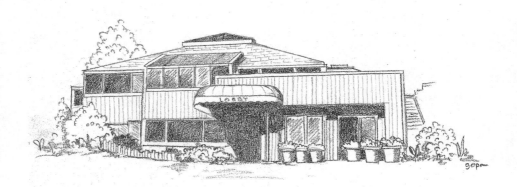

Elfriede's Beach Haus

Elfriede's Beach Haus
59 Brighton Avenue
Bolinas, CA 94924
(415) 868-9778

Room Rates:	$65–$149, AAA, AARP, AKC and ABA discounts.
Pet Charges or Deposits:	$10 per stay; manager's approval required.
Rated: 3 Paws 🐾🐾🐾	3 large rooms with brass and canopy beds, main parlor with fireplace, deck and garden with fountain.

Built in 1900 and restored in 1988, Elfriede's Beach Haus Bed and Breakfast charms guests with large, cozy rooms with plump down comforters. Breakfast is a celebration of wholesome foods prepared by the Bavarian innkeeper in a kitchen that resembles an artist's studio.

Guests are encouraged to spend the evening relaxing and visiting with others in the main parlor by the large Swiss fireplace. Surrounded by abundant wildlife, yet only minutes from the beach, tennis or hiking, guests may choose to spend their day relaxing on the deck, strolling through the lush garden, taking a "wild edible herb walk" or striking out with their dog for a day of sightseeing in this pet friendly town, where leash laws do not exist.

Anderson Creek Inn Bed and Breakfast

Anderson Creek Inn Bed and Breakfast
12050 Anderson Valley Way
Boonville, CA 95415
800-LLAMA-02
(707) 895-3091

Room Rates:	$95–$165
Pet Charges or Deposits:	$20; manager's approval required.
Rated: 3 Paws 🐾🐾🐾	5 spacious, elegant rooms, pool, spectacular views, near Hendy Woods State Park, close to town and wine tasting.

I n a small scenic valley on the way to the Mendocino Coast, visitors will discover the Anderson Creek Inn that blends the flavor of the area with comfortable elegance. Located on 16 acres at the fork of two creeks, this bed and breakfast inn offers guests convenient proximity to Highway 128 with enough seclusion for a quiet retreat.

The inn features five spacious rooms, each with king-sized beds, private bath and views of the valley's golden hills, peppered with ancient oaks and tall redwoods.

Arise to the fragrance of summer flowers mingling with the aroma of fresh ground coffee. Breakfast has become a special event at the Anderson Creek Inn, where every plate is a delicious work of art. It is the perfect opportunity to leisurely plan your day for a bike ride into town, a wine-tasting tour, a swim in the pool or an afternoon nap in the hammock for two.

Airport Doubletree Hotel

Airport Doubletree Hotel
835 Airport Boulevard
Burlingame, CA 94010
800-222-TREE
(415) 344-5500

Room Rates: $79, AAA and AARP discounts.
Pet Charges or Deposits: $20; manager's approval required.
Rated: 3 Paws 🐾🐾🐾 291 rooms and suites, many with bay views, coffee maker, hairdryer, iron and board, data ports, meeting and banquet facilities, catering services, concierge services, airport shuttle, laundry and valet services, library, fitness center, 24-hour room service, restaurant and lounge, bayside walking-jogging path, park nearby.

O verlooking the glistening waters of the San Francisco Bay and only minutes from the airport and many famous attractions is the Airport Doubletree Hotel. Each room and suite is highlighted by European decor, featuring amenities such as coffee maker, hairdryer, iron and board and data ports.

Guests are encouraged to browse the varied collection of books in the hotel library, which includes full concierge service and business center with secretarial services. The health and fitness center is equipped for a full workout, which can be supplemented with a jog or walk on the bayside trail with your dog.

The Chutney Grill serves breakfast and lunch, but is best known for its sizzling steaks. Relax after dinner with a cocktail at the Chutney Lounge.

The Pink Mansion

The Pink Mansion
1415 Foothill Boulevard
Calistoga, CA 94515
800-238-7465
(707) 942-0558

Room Rates:	$95–$175, breakfast included.
Pet Charges or Deposits:	$15 per day
Rated: 3 Paws 🐾🐾🐾	6 intimate rooms and suites, each with private baths, some with fireplaces, valley or forest views, indoor heated pool, large Victorian parlor, common drawing room, dining room and breakfast area, lavish breakfast and afternoon wine tasting, within walking distance to town and near many wineries.

Combining turn-of-the-century elegance with modern amenities, the Pink Mansion is a restored 1875 home in keeping with the spirit of the last resident, Aunt Alma Simic. Under her care in the 1930s, the house was repainted pink and christened the Pink Mansion, now a landmark in Calistoga.

Choose the large Victorian-style Rose Room Suite with a sunken sitting room and raised hearth fireplace or the Garden Room with its light airiness and panoramic view of Mt. St. Helena and the Palisades. The Angel Room is set in the corner of the mansion and features pieces from Aunt Alma's personal collection of angels. The Wine Suite is a secluded haven featuring wine collections, a custom made "Napa Bed" and a fireplace. The Forest Room is a wonderful retreat with antique furnishings and a view of the forest. The Oriental Room, decorated in mauve tones and Asian antiques, has a small sun deck with views of the forest.

You and your pet will enjoy the large garden areas and landscaped grounds.

Triple-S-Ranch

Triple-S-Ranch
4600 Mt. Home Ranch Road
Calistoga, CA 94515
(707) 942-6730

Room Rates:	$45–$65, an additional $7 per person
Pet Charges or Deposits:	$25 charge
Rated: 3 Paws 🐾 🐾 🐾	9 cabins with bathrooms, linens, swimming pool, horseshoes, bocci, restaurant and cocktails. Open April 1 to Dec. 31.

If you are looking for charming, rustic cabins when visiting the Calistoga area, the Triple-S-Ranch is a popular getaway. Located only three miles from town in the Sonoma Mountains, the ranch offers guests a chance to step back in time. Your accommodations include a furnished cabin, complete with linens, but there are no telephones, televisions or cooking facilities, except for the barbecue areas.

For your recreational pleasure there are horseshoes, bocci and a heated pool. If you enjoy wine tasting, visit some of the tasting rooms and local wineries in the area. Your dog will appreciate all of the open space surrounding the ranch, offering plenty of room for a hike and an opportunity to explore the outdoors in the heart of the Sonoma Mountains.

At mealtime, find your way to the legendary Triple-S-Ranch Restaurant and Bar, known for its onion rings and serving up everything from steak and lobster to hamburgers. The dress is casual and the portions are large.

Washington Street Lodging

Washington Street Lodging
1605 Washington Street
Calistoga, CA 94515
(707) 942-6968

Room Rates:	$105, includes continental breakfast.
Pet Charges or Deposits:	$15 per stay; manager's approval required.
Rated: 3 Paws ❀❀❀	5 cottages with full or partial kitchen, some with decks, television.

When looking for a secluded, riverside setting, try one of the private cottages at Washington Street Lodging. Here you will enjoy a cozy, country decor with many extra touches to make you feel right at home. Each of the five cottages offers guests a private bath and a full or partial kitchen. Enjoy a continental breakfast served in your room before heading off for a day of wine tasting or sightseeing in nearby downtown Calistoga.

Located within walking distance to the Napa River, you and your pet can hike along the riverbank or pack a picnic lunch and spend the afternoon in nature. Pets are welcome with manager's approval.

Cameron Park Inn – Best Western

Cameron Park Inn – Best Western
3361 Coach Lane
Cameron Park, CA 95682
800-601-1234
(916) 677-2203

Room Rates:	$60–$70, continental breakfast included, AAA and AARP discounts.
Rated: 3 Paws ❧❧❧	63 spacious rooms, some with kitchens, heated swimming pool and laundry facilities.

Located in the historic gold country between Sacramento and Placerville is the Cameron Park Inn – Best Western. Here guests may choose to relax by the heated swimming pool, head out for a day of wine tasting at one of the local wineries or explore the gold country and historic towns where you can spend the day trying to strike it rich by panning for gold.

For truly adventurous vacationers, there is white-water rafting at South Fork American River. Or at near by Folsom Lake, spend the day fishing or boating. If golf is your game, hit the links at the nearby course. The Eldorado National Forest offers you and your pet plenty of room to roam and explore the great outdoors.

Lakeside Chalets

Lakeside Chalets
5240 N. Lake Boulevard
Carnelian Bay, CA 96140
800-294-6378
(916) 546-5857

Room Rates:	$95–$145
Pet Charges or Deposits:	$40 deposit
Rated: 3 Paws 🐾🐾🐾	6 chalet cabins with fireplace, living room, fully equipped kitchen, dishwasher, cable TV, barbecue and panoramic views. Weekly rates available.

Waterfront chalets with stone fireplaces await you at Lakeside Chalets on the North Shore of Lake Tahoe. Here cozy cabins offer guests and their pets homey, comfortable accommodations with conveniences such as a fully equipped kitchen with dishwasher, a large master bedroom and a smaller bedroom with bunk beds.

Relax under the canopy of surrounding pine trees or drop a line in the water for a little fishing and to catch a little R&R. Other water sports include windsurfing, water skiing, sailing and boating. If you're a winter visitor, you're only minutes away from downhill and cross-country skiing or snowmobiling at Incline, Alpine Meadows, Northstar, Slide Mountain, Mt. Rose and Sugar Bowl. For gaming fans, Nevada casinos are only 10 minutes away.

Holiday Inn

Holiday Inn
685 Manzanita Court
Chico, CA 95926
800-310-2491 (CA only)
800-465-4329
(916) 345-2491

Room Rates:	$59, AAA and AARP discounts.
Pet Charges or Deposits:	$25
Rated: 3 Paws 🐾🐾🐾	172 guest rooms and suites, outdoor pool, whirlpool, complimentary airport shuttle, banquet and conference facilities, complimentary morning coffee, restaurant and cocktail lounge with live entertainment and complimentary buffet.

T he Holiday Inn is within two miles of California State University, Chico, Bidwell Mansion and State Historic Park. Chico's only full-service hotel is affordable and centrally located to both commercial and rural areas for antique shopping, touring breweries or hiking the wilds.

Molly Gunn's Restaurant serves up a varied menu while Molly Gunn's Bar was voted the area's "Best Happy Hour," offering a 25-foot-long complimentary buffet, nightly drink specials and dancing.

If you are looking for a nearby picnic spot or a place to spend the day with your pooch, the Bidwell Mansion and State Historic Park has more than 2,000 acres to explore.

Golden Lotus Bed and Breakfast Inn

Golden Lotus Bed and Breakfast Inn
1006 Lotus Road
Colma, CA 95613
(916) 621-4562

Room Rates:	$85–$125, breakfast included.
Pet Charges or Deposits:	$20 per day and $100 per animal deposit
Rated: 3 Paws 🐾🐾🐾	2 cottages with separate bath and 6 inn rooms with private baths, full library, sitting areas, veranda, flower and herb gardens, restaurant.

An old Indian campground on the American River is the site of the enchanting Golden Lotus Bed and Breakfast Inn. The main inn consists of six charming rooms. The Westward Ho room reflects the old west. The Orient Express takes you to China with an Asian flavor. The Secret Garden is a secluded room with cheery wicker furniture. Wish Upon takes you away to greet the magic genie. Pirates Cove whisks you away on Persian rugs. Tranquility boasts a relaxing, English cottage motif with soft colors. The two cottages that allow pets are The Honeysuckle, with two rooms separated by a bath, a mini kitchen and a floral and wicker decor; and The Hideaway, which consists of three small rooms and a full bath in a Southwestern decor.

For your dining pleasure, the historic Adam's Red Brick Restaurant is next to the inn and offers a varied menu plus desserts.

Sheraton Hotel and Conference Center

Sheraton Hotel and Conference Center
45 John Glenn Drive
Concord, CA 94520
800-325-3535
(510) 825-7700

Room Rates:	$70–$275, AAA, AARP, AKC and ABA discounts.
Pet Charges or Deposits:	Credit card imprint as deposit.
Rated: 4 Paws 🐾🐾🐾🐾	325 guest rooms and suites, some with refrigerators, valet laundry, Executive Club floor, indoor pool, spa, putting green, golf course, exercise room, restaurant and lounge with nightly entertainment, close to area attractions.

T he Sheraton Concord sports a refashioned exterior and new touches inside as well. Guest rooms and suites feature remote-control television, in-room coffee maker, two telephones, data port hookup and, for the business traveler, an oversized work station. Guests may enjoy the indoor pool, spa, exercise room or the putting green in the enclosed tropical garden atrium with its flowing streams and koi ponds. For die-hard golfers, the Buchanan Field Golf Course is adjacent to the hotel.

The new Executive Club level caters to the business traveler with upgraded services and amenities, an exclusive club-like atmosphere, a complimentary continental breakfast and hors d' oeuvres served in the evening.

Greenwood Pier Inn

Greenwood Pier Inn
5928 South Highway 1
Elk, CA 95432
(707) 877-9997

Room Rates:	$110–$225, including continental breakfast.
Pet Charges or Deposits:	$12 per day; manager's approval required.
Rated: 3 Paws 🐾🐾🐾	Rooms, cabins and cottages, many with panoramic views, fireplaces, spas, restaurant and room service.

Perched atop an ocean bluff with myriad rock formations and panoramic views in the old lumber town of Elk, the Greenwood Pier Inn dubs itself a "garden-by-the-edge-of-the-sea that grows flowers for your room."

Though your choice of accommodations is varied in this quirky complex of fairy-tale cottages, no matter which you choose it will include a private bath, fireplace and handmade quilts on a comfortable bed. Guests can relax on the deck with a glass of wine and scan the sea for an occasional whale spouting, watch the sea gulls soar through the sky as the seals sun themselves on the rocks below and fog gently rolls in.

The new Café is open daily, offering creative dinners of local seafood accompanied by fresh veggies from the inn's garden. The flower-bordered paths and seaside gardens are the perfect settings for celebrations or simply for a stroll.

The Eureka Inn

The Eureka Inn
518 Seventh Street
Eureka, CA 95501
800-862-4906
(707) 442-6441

Room Rates: $89–$250, AAA, AARP and AKC discounts.
Rated: 4 Paws 🐾🐾🐾🐾 105 rooms and luxury suites, fireplaces, wet bars, kitchens, formal dining areas, valet laundry, Jacuzzi tub, sauna, heated pool, restaurants and lounges.

T he Eureka Inn is set like a gem in one of California's most magnificent natural environments. Forests of towering redwoods, miles of wave-washed shore and cascading mountain streams offer endless allure.

Since 1922, the inn has enchanted guests with its elegance, sophistication, European flair and Tudor styling. You can almost hear the footsteps of history on the polished hardwood floors. A National Historic Place, the inn's lofty ceilings, redwood beams and baronial half-timbering exude classic English manor house richness.

Relax in the deep leather settees by the inviting fire in the Grand Lobby before enjoying the inn's tradition of fine dining in a variety of restaurants and lounges, which range from the intimately elegant to the eclectic. Venturing out can mean exploring a fern-shrouded canyon, standing beneath the world's tallest tree or greeting fishing boats as they return to harbor.

Country Inn – Best Western

Country Inn – Best Western
1528 Kenmar Road
Fortuna, CA 95540
800-679-7511
(707) 725-6822

Room Rates:	$58-$115, AAA, AARP and AKC discounts.
Pet Charges or Deposits:	$20 deposit; notify manager.
Rated: 3 Paws 🐾🐾🐾	66 rooms, indoor-outdoor pool, indoor whirlpool, laundry facilities, microwaves and refrigerators.

T his country resort inn was voted USA Today Readers Choice Award for the "Best Weekend Getaway." The 66-unit inn is set in the heart of the Redwood Empire near North Coast attractions, including the Eel and Van Duzen rivers that lure anglers for a bit of salmon and steelhead fishing.

Guests can relax in the indoor whirlpool or take a swim in the 83-degree swimming pool in a setting that affords picture-window views to the lush landscaped grounds.

For other leisure pursuits, the inn is within minutes of Victorian Ferndale, Scotia Sawmill Tour, Avenue of the Giants as well as ocean beaches, parks and restaurants.

Residence Inn by Marriott

Residence Inn by Marriott
5400 Farwell Place
Fremont, CA 94536
800-331-3131
(510) 794-5900

Room Rates:	$99–$169, including breakfast. Call for discounts.
Pet Charges or Deposits:	$10 per stay; $75 cleaning fee.
Rated: 3 Paws 🐾🐾🐾	80 rooms and suites, all with living rooms and separate sleeping areas, full kitchen, some with fireplaces, meeting facilities, 2 heated pools, whirlpool, sports court, cable television, VCR and movie library, complimentary evening beverages, laundry facilities, airport transportation and pet exercise area.

T ravelers will appreciate the comforts and conveniences offered at the Fremont – Residence Inn by Marriott. The accommodations are spacious with separate sleeping and living areas with wood-burning fireplaces. Amenities include fully equipped kitchens, daily maid service, laundry facilities as well as room service from any of the local restaurants. A hosted continental breakfast buffet and informal hospitality happy hour are included.

The Residence Inn by Marriott offers a heated swimming pool, two whirlpools, three barbecue areas, a sports court where you can play a game of basketball, volleyball or tennis and landscaped grounds for a stroll with your dog.

Isis Oasis Lodge

Isis Oasis Lodge
20889 Geyserville Avenue
Geyserville, CA 95441
800-679-PETS
(707) 857-3524

Room Rates:	$45–$200, includes full breakfast.
Rated: 3 Paws 🐾🐾🐾	Lodge with 12 private rooms and shared baths; retreat house that sleeps up to 15; a four-bedroom house with two baths, full kitchen and fireplaces; and 2 cottages, one with full kitchen and private hot tub.

If you are looking for a magical retreat for the mind and body when visiting the wine country, try the Isis Oasis Lodge. The Lodge has 12 private rooms with Egyptian motif and shared baths. The Retreat House is a three-bedroom, three-bath house that sleeps up to 15. The Tower is a small cottage with a view and private half-bath and shower. The Vineyard House has four bedrooms, two fireplaces, full kitchen and scenic views. The Isis Suite is a Victorian bedroom and sitting room with private bath. The Wine Barrel Room, Tipi and Pyramid are alternative style rooms with a bathhouse.

The lodge is located on ancient Pomo Indian ceremonial grounds. It has been a gathering place for groups and individuals seeking an extraordinary experience for years. Guests may spend the day hiking, swimming in the heated pool, relaxing in one of the patio areas, taking wine-tasting tours or visiting the many resident animals. Located near the river, there is plenty of open space for you and your dog to explore.

The Big Dog Inn

closed

The Big Dog Inn
15244 Arnold Drive
Glen Ellen, CA 95442
(707) 996-4319

Room Rates: $100–$150, breakfast included.
Rated: 4 Paws 🐾🐾🐾🐾 Guest Cottage and in-house suite, both with private baths.

estled among six acres of rolling hills in historic Sonoma Valley, the Big Dog Inn blends history and hospitality in the heart of California's famed wine country.

The cathedral-ceiling guest cottage with sitting room, country furnishings and wood-burning stove offers exquisite views of the Sonoma Valley. The in-house suite features two bedrooms and a private sitting room. The patio, pool and spa areas reward travel weary visitors with a chance for a relaxing pause after a full day of sightseeing, touring local wineries or shopping. For adventuresome guests, the area boasts miles of hiking, biking and horseback riding trails for you and your dog to enjoy at Jack London State Park.

Innkeepers Penny and Doug Mahon have raised and shown St. Bernards for more than 30 years and welcome guests to tour the kennel building for an up-close and personal Big Dog Inn experience.

Gray Eagle Lodge

Gray Eagle Lodge
Graeagle, CA 96103
800-635-8778
(916) 836-2511

www.grayeaglelodge

Room Rates:	$145–$190, including breakfast, dinner and daily maid service.
Pet Charges or Deposits:	$10 per day; dogs only.
Rated: 3 Paws 🐾🐾🐾	18 cabins with full bath (showers only) and refrigerator, many outdoor activities, game room, restaurant, bar and gift shop.

Merely step out of the door and the adventure begins at the Gray Eagle Lodge where miles of trails lead to meadows and ponds, ridges and peaks and alpine lakes galore. And should you anglers come back with a "big one"—a fish or a fish tale—the inn keeps champagne on ice to reward the best fish stories.

Established in 1923, the family-owned-and-operated lodge offers guest their choice of 18 rustic cabins with full baths. There are no cooking facilities, but the room rate includes breakfast and dinner. The dinner menu offers daily selections ranging from pan-seared rainbow trout, medallions of pork tenderloins to slow-roasted Long Island duckling. For a small fee, the chef will gladly prepare a picnic lunch or even cook up your catch of the day.

This "dog friendly" lodge is set among 1 million acres of the Plumas National Forest that includes the Feather River, several lakes, recreation areas and plenty of room to roam. The Gray Eagle Creek is next to the lodge and affords fishing and rafting fun. Gray Eagle Falls spills into a pond, creating an inviting swimming hole. Add mountain biking, hiking, two golf courses and horse stables nearby, what more could you ask for? How about no phones and televisions as distractions.

Madrona Manor

Madrona Manor
1001 Westside Road
Healdsburg, CA 95448
800-258-4003
(707) 433-4231

Room Rates: $145–$245, includes full breakfast.
Pet Charges or Deposits: $30 deposit; manager's approval required.
Rated: 5 Paws 🐾🐾🐾🐾🐾 18 rooms and 3 suites, air-conditioned, most with fireplaces, some with balcony and decks, swimming pool.

When looking for accommodations with landscaped grounds, concierge service and conference facilities while maintaining a sense of homey elegance, look no further than the Madrona Manor. The staff strives to make guests feel at home in the 21 Victorian-style rooms, many with fireplaces.

Start your day off with the expansive, complimentary breakfast buffet, then curl up with a captivating book by the fire in one of the common rooms, tastefully decorated in period antiques accented with handmade Persian carpets.

You and your dog will likely be tempted to take a stroll in the impeccably landscaped gardens or explore the wooded acreage. Whatever you choose to do, make sure to end your day with an elegant candlelight dinner prepared by Chef Todd Muir, served in one of the three dining rooms.

Sorensen's Resort

Sorensen's Resort
14255 Highway 88
Hope Valley, CA 96120
800-423-9949
(916) 694-2203

Room Rates:	$70–$275
Pet Charges or Deposits:	Room rate as deposit; two-pet limit; allowed only in certain cabins.
Rated: 3 Paws 🐾🐾🐾	3 bed-and-breakfast rooms and 27 cottages and cabins with fireplace or wood-burning stoves, sitting areas, full kitchens and sleeping accommodations for up to 6.

C lose to more than 100 lakes, streams and some of the best skiing in the Sierras you'll discover Sorensen's and Hope Valley Resort. Here you'll find a romantic hideaway or a hostel for your ski trip with friends and family. The amenities, activities, and down-home hospitality make guests feel right at home. The cozy Country Café is perfect for a warm brew or a cozy meal. There are plenty of activities to keep you busy, including the classes and guide service from the Horse Feathers Fly Fishing School, river rafting tours and ski instructions from Hope Valley Cross Country Ski Center.

The Ark

firtree cottage?

The Ark
180 Highland Way
Inverness, CA 94937
(415) 663-9338

Room Rates:	$130, breakfast included.
Pet Charges or Deposits:	$10 per stay
Rated: 4 Paws 🐾🐾🐾🐾	Cottage for 2 to 6 guests, full kitchen.

Tucked away in the forest a mile up the ridge from the village of Inverness, The Ark is a romantic private hideaway an hour north of the Golden Gate Bridge, next to the magnificent Point Reyes National Seashore.

Built and named in 1971 by a class of UC Berkeley architecture students, The Ark offers seclusion in the form of a charming two-room cottage with a spacious main room with a wood-burning stove and overlooking the forest. The cozy comfortable furnishings include original works of local artists.

Recreational options include whale-watching, horseback riding or taking a leisurely walk on the beach with your dog. Just down the road are the marshy headwaters of Tomales Bay, a noted place for bird watching. If you're feeling especially adventurous, try the Papermill Creek for rafting and kayaking.

Dancing Coyote Beach

Dancing Coyote Beach
12794 Sir Francis Drake Boulevard
Inverness, CA 94937
(415) 669-7200

Room Rates:	$95–$125, AAA, AARP, AKC and American Airlines discounts.
Rated: 4 Paws 🐾🐾🐾🐾	4 cottages with galley kitchens, skylights, fireplaces and bay views.

Dancing Coyote Beach delivers privacy and bed-and-breakfast charm, only 80 minutes from the cultural energy of San Francisco. Situated in the midst of the Point Reyes National Seashore, Dancing Coyote Beach offers a convenient home base for bicycling, hiking, whale watching, birding and beach-combing.

Each of the four cottages has a galley kitchen, skylights, fireplace and views of the bay. For dining, enjoy breakfast on your own private deck in the morning sun or a romantic fireside dinner at night or wander into sleepy Inverness to sample the menus of several fine restaurants.

This place is a quiet retreat, free of the noise of electronics and bustle, so guests are encouraged to stroll along the sandy beach following the graceful curve of the shoreline or to heed the call of sheltering pines and cedars and warm, sunny spots.

Rosemary Cottage

Rosemary Cottage
75 Balboa Avenue
Inverness, CA 94937
(415) 663-9338

Room Rates:	$160, including breakfast.
Pet Charges or Deposits:	$10 per stay
Rated: 5 Paws 🐾🐾🐾🐾🐾	Cottage for two to four guests, views of Point Reyes National Seashore.

L ocated on the Inverness Ridge, Rosemary Cottage is a romantic French-country "pied-a-terre." A wall of windows provides a dramatic forest view in the Point Reyes National Seashore. A large deck under an aging oak overlooks the herb garden in this secluded hideaway.

Guests will appreciate the many hand-crafted details, large bedroom, high ceilings and wood-burning stove.

Only minutes from the beach, travelers can enjoy fishing, boating, whale watching, horseback riding or a walk on the beach with your dog. Miles of hiking trails in the Point Reyes National Seashore are only 10 minutes from the cottage. Just down the road are the marshy headwaters of Tomales Bay, a great place for bird watching. For rafting or kayaking, try Papermill Creek. If you would prefer to just relax, stay at the cottage and soak in the garden hot tub.

The Tree House Bed and Breakfast

The Tree House Bed and Breakfast
Inverness – Point Reyes Station, CA 94956
800-495-8720
(415) 663-8720

Room Rates: $100–$125, includes continental breakfast.
Pet Charges or Deposits: None; all pets are welcome.
Rated: 5 Paws 🐾🐾🐾🐾🐾   3 private rooms, with separate entry and private bath.

Located one hour from either Santa Rosa or San Francisco, The Tree House Bed and Breakfast at Inverness on Point Reyes is a secluded destination for a weekend retreat or a relaxing vacation. Select from three private rooms. The Princess Room is furnished in antiques and a brass bed. The Queen Quarters, attached to the main house with its own private entry, comes with a wet bar, private bathroom, queen-size bed, fireplace and views of the valley. The Kings Room, complete with private bath and king-size bed, offers a private balcony and an expansive mountain view. All accommodations include a continental breakfast.

Once you are settled in your room, take your dog and head out for a day of hiking and bird watching at nearby Point Reyes National Seashore and Golden Gate Recreation Area.

The Stanford Inn by the Sea

The Stanford Inn by the Sea
Coast Highway 1 and Comptche Ukiah Road
Mendocino, CA 95460
800-331-8884
(707) 937-5025

Room Rates: $175–$275, includes breakfast.
Pet Charges or Deposits: $25 per stay
Rated: 5 Paws 🐾🐾🐾🐾🐾 23-room bed and breakfast inn, furnished with antiques,
                      "welcome" gifts for pets at check-in.

Set in historic gardens between coastal forest and the Pacific Ocean is The Stanford Inn by the Sea. A small certified organic working garden and farm, the 23-room inn embodies the best of the rugged Mendocino Coast. The inn offers a buffet champagne breakfast and organic meals, along with amenities found in a fine hotel, while maintaining a cozy, homey feeling.

Rooms paneled with pine or redwood and decorated with antiques, plants and art from local artists make you want to linger by the fire just a little longer before heading out.

Pets are most welcome here. At check-in, your dog will receive biscuits, water and food bowls and bedding. But be forewarned, there are animals living on the premises: two horses, 14 llamas, swans, a goose, ducks, three dogs and 11 cats.

The Tree House – Best Western Motor Inn

The Tree House – Best Western Motor Inn
III Morgan Way
Mount Shasta, CA 96067
800-545-7164
(916) 928-3101

Room Rates:	$74–$160, AAA and AARP discounts.
Pet Charges or Deposits:	None; small pets only.
Rated: 3 Paws 🐾 🐾 🐾	95 rooms and deluxe suites, landscaped grounds, heated indoor pool, some refrigerators, views of Mount Shasta, banquet and convention facilities, fully equipped business center, restaurant and cocktail lounge.

Perched in the shadow of Mount Shasta is The Tree House – Best Western Motor Inn, where hospitality complements the rustic elegance of the inn. The warm glow of the natural wood paneling in the rooms, gourmet dining, the cozy warmth of the fireplace in the cocktail lounge, the view overlooking the majestic mountain and the serene atmosphere of the inn all add up to a relaxing stay.

The indoor heated pool is perfect for a dip anytime of the year. Enjoy skiing and snow sports in the winter. When the weather warms up, there's plenty of fishing areas and water sports to keep you busy.

Holiday Harbor Resort and Marina

Holiday Harbor Resort and Marina
20061 Shasta Caverns Road
O'Brien, CA 96070
800-776-2628
(916) 238-2383

Room Rates: $300–$540

Rated: 3 Paws ❀❀❀   7 houseboats, all-weather cabin, railed walkways, range and oven, refrigerator, ice chest, cabin heater, 12-volt light system, shower, bunk beds, gas grill, RV park and campground.

Just imagine cruising around scenic Shasta Lake with the whole family, including your pet, enjoying all the comforts of home aboard your own houseboat.

Much of what you need is provided, just bring your food, linens, games, grilling utensils and bathing suits. The staff will instruct you on the operating procedures of your houseboat. The Toy Box Rental Center has everything you need to rent from fishing boats to Jet Skis.

The campgrounds have 27 tree-studded sites with full hook-up by the water. There are laundry facilities, showers, restrooms, private docking for boats and a swimming area. Advanced reservations are required for tent camping.

Heritage Inn – Best Western

Heritage Inn – Best Western
11269 Point East Drive
Rancho Cordova, CA 95742
800-641-1076
(916) 635-4040

Room Rates:	$59–$79 buffet breakfast included, AAA, AARP and AKC discounts.
Pet Charges or Deposits:	$15 deposit
Rated: 3 Paws ❀❀❀	124 rooms and deluxe king suites, pool, sauna, fitness center.

Whether looking for outlet shopping, wine sipping or outdoor adventures, travelers will find that The Best Western Heritage Inn offers an array of amenities and recreational opportunities. All rooms include coffee makers, hairdryers and refrigerators. The deluxe king leisure suites have spacious living and bar areas. A complimentary breakfast buffet and manager's reception are offered daily

You and your dog can strike out for a bit of exploring along trails at American River, Folsom Lake and Lake Natoma. Pet sitters are available if you wish to take in some of the local history or venture to area factory outlets or wineries.

Doubletree Hotel

Doubletree Hotel
1 Doubletree Drive
Rohnert Park, CA 94928
800-222-TREE
(707) 584-5466

Room Rates:	$84 and up, AAA, AARP, AKC and ABA discounts.
Pet Charges or Deposits:	$100 deposit
Rated: 4 Paws 🐾🐾🐾🐾	245 rooms and suites, heated pool, whirlpool, tennis courts, 36-hole golf course, exercise room, banquet facilities, restaurants, coffee shop and cocktail lounge.

L ocated near the scenic Sonoma County wine country is the Spanish Mission-style Rohnert Park – Sonoma County Doubletree Hotel. Guests will appreciate the amenities of spacious rooms and suites of this first-class hotel. The friendly staff will see to your every need and greet you upon arrival with their signature greeting of freshly baked chocolate chip cookies.

Spend your day utilizing the hotel's many recreational amenities or venture out to discover your own. The two hotel restaurants feature a varied menu lineup.

There is plenty of room for your dog to roam on the landscaped, waterfront grounds, plus there are several historic parks in the vicinity as well.

Red Lion Inn

Red Lion Inn
1401 Arden Way
Sacramento, CA 95815
800-733-5466
(916) 922-8041

Room Rates:	$79–$114, AAA and AARP discounts.
Pet Charges or Deposits:	$50 deposit; manager's approval required.
Rated: 3 Paws 🐾🐾🐾	376 large rooms and 8 luxury suites, some with patios or balconies and refrigerators, conference facilities, putting green, 3 pools, wading pool, exercise room, guest laundry service, gift shop, room service, restaurants and cocktail lounge.

L ocated only minutes from the center of the city, the Sacramento – Red Lion Inn offers guest easy access to downtown, the state capitol, as well as the entire Sacramento area. Here guests will enjoy spacious accommodations, complete with air conditioning, large work areas and meeting facilities for the business traveler, laundry and valet services and other luxuries.

After a day of sightseeing or business meetings, relax by one of the three pools, go for a stroll around the spacious grounds with your dog or indulge in a workout in the fully equipped exercise room.

For casual dining, have your meal poolside at the covered barbecue and bar, opt for the relaxing ambiance of the Coffee Garden or grab a quick bite at the lobby's Espresso Bar and Deli. After dinner, unwind with some hot jazz at Savanna's Lounge.

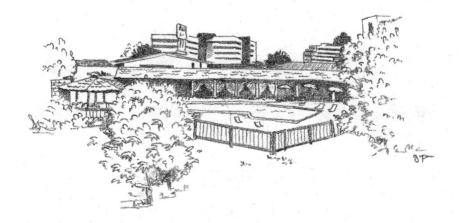

Airport Hilton Hotel

Airport Hilton Hotel
San Francisco International Airport
San Francisco, CA 94128
800-HILTONS
(415) 589-0770

Room Rates:	$149–$189
Pet Charges or Deposits:	None; must sign waiver; small pets only.
Rated: 4 Paws 🐾🐾🐾🐾	527 oversized rooms, some with balconies, in-room refreshment center, coffee maker, pool, garden courtyard, work centers, meeting and banquet facilities, airport shuttle and exercise area for dogs.

The San Francisco Airport Hilton Hotel is the only hotel located directly on the airport grounds. This luxury hotel offers guests oversized rooms, with in-room refreshment centers, work areas and secretarial services. Many of the rooms have balconies overlooking the courtyard or the pool.

Before or after your trip, enjoy a workout in the fitness center, take your dog for a leisurely stroll through the garden courtyard or simply relax at the Olympic-sized heated pool.

Dining options range from the intimate English country inn setting of the Barronshire Restaurant serving fine continental cuisine to casual fare at Café Café. Don't forget the Lobby Bar with its big-screen television to catch up on sporting events or end your day with a cocktail by the grand piano.

Airport Westin Hotel

San Francisco Airport Westin Hotel
1 Old Bayshore Highway
Millbrae, CA 94030
800-228-3000
(415) 692-3500

Room Rates:	$94–$190
Pet Charges or Deposits:	$75 cleaning fee; pets under 35 pounds.
Rated: 3 Paws 🐾🐾🐾	390 rooms, many with bay views, landscaped grounds, in-room refreshment center, business center, conference facilities, heated indoor pool, saunas, whirlpool, fitness center, 24-hour room service, restaurant and lounge, coffee and gift shop, across from Bayfront Park.

S an Francisco's waterfront is home to the San Francisco Airport – Westin Hotel. Located just two minutes from the airport and 15 minutes from downtown, business travelers and vacationers alike appreciate the convenience of this resort-like hotel. Amenities include 390 luxury rooms, many with bay views.

The fitness-minded should check out the hotel's fully equipped fitness center or grab the leash and take your dog for a run on the six-mile jogging trail at the Bayfront Park across the street from the hotel.

Hungry for Mediterranean food? The Alfiere Restaurant is a bistro featuring exotic cuisine in a relaxing setting. The Lobby Lounge and The Bar are perfect for a casual business meeting or get-together with friends. If you find you left a few essential items at home, stop by The Runway Coffee and Gift Shop for various sundries or a hot cup of java.

Campton Place Hotel

Campton Place Hotel
340 Stockton Street
San Francisco, CA 94108
800-235-4300
(415) 781-5555

Room Rates:	$225–$980, AAA, AARP, AKC and ABA discounts.
Pet Charges or Deposits:	$25 per day; pets up to 40 pounds.
Rated: 5 Paws 🐾🐾🐾🐾🐾	117 rooms, concierge, acclaimed restuarant, five-star amenities, convenient to shopping, business, dining and entertainment.

Just steps from San Francisco's Union Square and a step up from most hotels is one of the truly luxurious hotels in the world—Campton Place.

The accommodations at the Campton Place Hotel frequent the list of the "Readers Choice Awards" of Conde Nast Travel magazine, which has ranked it "One of the top 25 U.S. hotels." The small niceties of a European inn combine with the polished precision of a grand hotel—concierge, newspaper delivery, thick robes, valet parking.

The elegant five-star restaurant at Campton Place continues to earn extraordinary acclaim. Diners enjoy award-winning cuisine, fine French and American wines and an ambiance graced by Wedgewood crystal and fresh flowers. The adjoining bar provides a cozy setting for afternoon tea or one of the hotel's famous dry martinis.

The Clift Hotel

The Clift Hotel
495 Geary Street
San Francisco, CA 94102
800-HERITAGE
(415) 929-2300

Room Rates:	$240 and up; AAA, AARP AKC and ABA discounts.
Pet Charges or Deposits:	$40 per room
Rated: 5 Paws 🐾🐾🐾🐾🐾	326 rooms and suites, business center, fitness center, 24-hour room service, overnight laundry and dry cleaning services, Guest Recognition Program and full-service concierge.

I n 1915, Fredrick C. Clift opened a hotel that rose out of the rubble of old San Francisco amid the futuristic fanfare of the Panama-Pacific Exposition, promising the grand tradition of days gone by while embracing America's growing world influence. The Clift Hotel has kept that promise. This 80-year-old "Grande Dame" has been impeccably maintained and continues to exude luxurious comfort.

Amid chandeliers and elegant decor, guests enjoy high-ranking service and amenities. Each room is decorated with fine linens and furnishings, with an attention to detail. With the staff at your service 24 hours a day, virtually everything is available to you with just one phone call, even chocolate cake and milk at midnight.

For award-winning California French cuisine, look no further than the gracious, romantic environment of The French Room. The Redwood Room is an Art Deco lounge and piano bar built from a 2,000-year-old giant redwood tree from Northern California. The redwood walls, 22-foot fluted columns and mural bar make this one of the most beautiful places in the world for cocktails.

The Mansions Hotel

The Mansions Hotel
2220 Sacramento Street
San Francisco, CA 94115
800-826-9398
(415) 929-9444

Room Rates:	$89–$225, including breakfast and nightly magic performance.
Pet Charges or Deposits:	None.
Rated: 3 Paws 🐾🐾🐾	21 rooms and suites, billiard/game room, historic museum, magic parlor, sculpture gardens and views of the Golden Gate Bridge. Restaurant.

T here's magic in the air in more ways than one at The Mansions Hotel and Restaurant in the heart of San Francisco. When you step into the grand foyer with the crystal chandeliers, the creaking of the gumwood walls and Bach's music playing in the parlor, you are whisked back in time. Surrounded by tapestries, paintings and historic memorabilia, every room is different. Some have a terrace with a view of the Golden Gate Bridge, but all guest rooms include a private bath, fresh flowers, California apples and a special arrival gift.

The Mansions restaurant and dinner theater is one of San Francisco's top 10 dinner spots, offering an assorted menu from a light buffet to a lavish banquet. Make your reservations early for an evening of entertainment. There are haunting nightly performances in the Victorian Cabaret by America's most acclaimed illusionists. Listen closely, can you hear the whispers of the resident ghost, Claudia?

Marriott Fisherman's Wharf

Marriott Fisherman's Wharf
1250 Columbus Avenue
San Francisco, CA 94133
800-831-4004
(415) 775-7555

Room Rates:	$139–$169, AAA discounts.
Pet Charges or Deposits:	None; small pets only.
Rated: 3 Paws 🐾🐾🐾	256 rooms with honor bars, some with refrigerators, meeting facilities, sauna, health club, valet service, restaurant and cocktail lounge.

Set in the heart of San Francisco's Northern Waterfront District is the renowned San Francisco—Marriott Fisherman's Wharf. From the moment you enter the hotel, you will be greeted by friendly staff and an inviting atmosphere and guest rooms packed with amenities.

With such a central location, you may want to venture out for a day of sightseeing on the wharf, take a ride on a cable car or a boat tour of the bay. Then wind down with a workout in the hotel's health club or relax in the spa before dining at the hotel's restaurant, Spada, featuring an intimate atmosphere and casual California cuisine. Top off your dinner with a nightcap at the quiet, sophisticated Lobby Lounge.

The hotel boasts an exercise area for your pet to stretch his legs or stop by the desk for directions to a nearby local park if you feel like exploring the city with your pooch.

Marriott Hotel

Marriott Hotel
55 Fourth Street
San Francisco, CA 94103
800-644-5008
(415) 896-1600

Room Rates: $139 and up, AAA, AARP, AKC and ABA discounts.
Rated: 4 Paws 🐾🐾🐾🐾   1,636 rooms and suites with honor bars, heated indoor pool, whirlpool, sauna, steam room, exercise room, massage by appointment, business center, conference facilities, secretarial services, laundry, valet parking, airport limousine service, car rental desk, activities desk, room service, coffee shop, restaurants and lounges.

I n the midst of historic San Francisco is the elegant San Francisco Marriott Hotel. This modern hotel offers all the amenities travelers expect in a four-star hotel. Guests will fine richly decorated rooms and luxury suites with such conveniences as individual climate controls, fire and personal safety systems and in-room mini bars.

Keep fit with an invigorating workout in the state-of-the-art health club, followed by a refreshing splash in the indoor pool or a relaxing soak in the whirlpool.

Sample the Garden Terrace's California cuisine and lavish buffets in a casual, family atmosphere. Kinoko features teppanyaki-style specialties prepared at your table. The Fourth Street Deli is a popular sports bar and offers light fare. The Atrium Lounge, located in the five-story atrium, serves cocktails and refreshments. Stop by the View Lounge for refreshments, cocktails and a spectacular view of the city.

Pan Pacific Hotel

Pan Pacific Hotel
500 Post Street
San Francisco, CA 94102
800-327-8585
(415) 771-8600

Room Rates:	$205 and up
Pet Charges or Deposits:	$25 per day; small pets only.
Rated: 4 Paws 🐾🐾🐾🐾	330 rooms and 19 suites, personal valet, chauffeur-driven Rolls Royce, business center, conference facilities, exercise room, 24-hour room service, restaurant and cocktail lounge.

San Francisco's Pan Pacific Hotel is synonymous with luxury and sophistication. Accommodations are augmented by a sumptuous bathroom with deep soaking tub, soft terry cloth robes and a personal valet to attend to your every need, including a chauffeur-driven Rolls Royce at your disposal.

The Pan Pacific Bar offers a compelling diversion to the bustling city below. The Pacific Restaurant has become a destination in itself, with its relaxing environment, soft piano music, the splash of the fountain and the crackle of the inviting fire.

The Westin St. Francis Hotel

The Westin St. Francis Hotel
335 Powell Street – Union Square
San Francisco, CA 94102
800-WESTIN-1
(415) 397-7000

Room Rates:	$199 and up
Pet Charges or Deposits:	None; dogs only.
Rated: 5 Paws 🐾🐾🐾🐾🐾	1,200 rooms and suites, in-room bars, business center, conference facilities, secretarial services, valet parking, exercise room, 2 dining rooms, coffee shop, cocktail lounge.

S ince 1904, the award-winning St. Francis Hotel has been known for its rich heritage. Located in the heart of San Francisco, the 1,200 impeccably appointed guest rooms and luxurious suites offer an array of amenities. Whether hosting a gala for kings or an intimate gathering, you will appreciate the meticulous attention to detail. The grandfather clock in the lobby is the perfect place to rendezvous before dining at one of the five renowned restaurants.

World famous Victor's offers a distinctive menu and breathtaking views 32 stories above the city. To partake of some of San Francisco's finest seafood, dine at the elegant, oak-paneled St. Francis Grill. Experience high tea and jazz in the opulent Compass Rose. To taste test some of the more than 50 beers from around the world, stop by Dewey's Pub. For an evenings entertainment among the stars, visit OZ, the premier dance club.

Villa Hotel

Villa Hotel
4000 El Camino Real
San Mateo, CA 94403
800-341-2345
(650) 341-0966

Room Rates:	$79–$115, AAA and AARP discounts.
Pet Charges or Deposits:	$50 deposit
Rated: 3 Paws 🐾🐾🐾	272 rooms and 14 suites, business center, conference and banquet facilities, heated pool, exercise room, restaurant, coffee shop, cocktail lounge with live entertainment, gift shop, beauty and barber shops and massage therapist.

Whether vacationing in the Bay Area or attending a convention or seminar, the Villa Hotel offers comfort and convenience. Located 20 minutes from San Francisco and Silicon Valley, the possibilities for adventure, recreation and relaxation for you and your pet abound.

A full slate of recreational and business services are available for the asking. For dining and beverages, choose the gourmet menu of the hotel restaurant, the causal atmosphere of the Villa Coffee House or an evening of entertainment in the cocktail lounge.

Residence Inn by Marriott

Residence Inn by Marriott
1071 Market Street
San Ramon, CA 94583
800-331-3131
(510) 277-9292

Room Rates:	$109–$189, including breakfast buffet, AAA and AARP discounts.
Pet Charges or Deposits:	$5 per day and $75 cleaning fee.
Rated: 3 Paws 🐾🐾🐾	106 rooms and suites, all with living rooms and separate sleeping areas, full kitchen, some with fireplaces, meeting facilities, cable television, VCR and movie library, 2 heated pools, whirlpool, sports court, complimentary evening beverages, laundry facilities, airport transportation and pet exercise area.

When it comes to comfortable and affordable lodging, San Ramon – Residence Inn by Marriott often garners top honors. Voted the "Gold Hotel" award and "1994 Hotel of the Year," the inn offers inviting touches such as wood-burning fireplaces, separate sleeping and living areas, breakfast buffet and complimentary hospitality hours.

Start your day with the breakfast buffet served at the Gatehouse, followed by a day of sightseeing, a visit to some of the major attractions or stay where you are and relax by the pool, swim a few laps or venture to the sports court for a game of tennis, volleyball or basket ball. You and your dog can take a walk around the landscaped grounds and exercise area. There are even dog runs available and a park is just across the street.

Inn at Heavenly Bed and Breakfast Lodge

Inn at Heavenly Bed and Breakfast
1261 Ski Run Boulevard
South Lake Tahoe, CA 96150
800-MY-CABIN
(916) 544-4244

Room Rates: $85–$165, AAA discounts.
Pet Charges or Deposits: $100 deposit; dogs only.
Rated: 4 Paws 🐾🐾🐾🐾   15-room bed and breakfast, some with kitchenettes, refrigerators and microwaves, private spa room, hot tub, sauna, steam room, separate cabins for parties of up to 16, lodge and park available for groups and weddings. Full-service wedding arrangements. Pets sitters available upon request.

Set on 1½ acres of woods in South Lake Tahoe, Inn at Heavenly Bed and Breakfast Lodge is a log cabin-style lodge with a knotty-pine interior and exterior with custom log furniture throughout.

Accommodations vary in size, some housing natural stone fireplaces, separate sitting areas, refrigerators and microwaves, but all offering large, homey rooms with patchwork quilts and views of the park. There is a private hot tub room, sauna and steam room available by reservation.

You and your canine pal will enjoy the park-like setting offering barbecue and picnic areas with log swings.

Harvest Inn

Harvest Inn
1 Main Street
St. Helena, CA 94574
800-950-8466
(707) 963-9463

Room Rates:	$99–$370, AAA and AARP discounts.
Pet Charges or Deposits:	$20 per pet per day.
Rated: 4 Paws 🐾🐾🐾🐾	54 rooms with wet bars and refrigerators, many with fireplaces, antique furnishings, English Tudor style, surrounded by gardens and vineyards, 2 swimming pools and whirlpool.

Nestled in the heart of Napa Valley are the charming, turn-of-the-century, English Tudor guest cottages of the Harvest Inn. The elegant but inviting guest rooms are reminiscent of the country gentry style of a bygone era. Many accommodations feature brick fireplaces, wet bars, refrigerators and are adorned with period antiques.

Reflecting the abundance of each season, colorful flowers and fruit-bearing trees grace lush lawns surrounding the inn's 14-acre working vineyard. Guests often stroll to the many neighboring wineries for tasting and guided tours. Forests and stately vineyards provide walking and/or jogging paths as part of many extras. Bicycle some of the most exciting routes in the Bay Area or hike the scenic hillsides and meadows of Bothe-Napa State Park. The renowned shops and restaurants of St. Helena are only a few minutes away.

Tahoe Keys Resort

Tahoe Keys Resort
599 Tahoe Keys Boulevard
Tahoe Keys Village, CA 96150
800-MY-TAHOE
(916) 544-5397

Room Rates: $100–$1,750 per night.
Pet Charges or Deposits: $25 per stay and $100 deposit.
Rated: 5 Paws 🐾🐾🐾🐾🐾   A private resort with waterfront condos, homes and villas. Front desk and concierge services, indoor and outdoor pool, spa, health club, lighted tennis courts, private beach; meeting, wedding and party facilities.

Tahoe Keys Resort is a 750-acre private resort at famed Lake Tahoe. This year-round resort offers waterfront vacation rentals of premier three- to six-bedroom homes, studios, condominiums and a VIP villa, all with views of the water or the surrounding mountains. All accommodations come with complete kitchens and fireplaces.

Tahoe Keys Resort is a complete destination resort at Lake Tahoe, featuring a waterfront restaurant, an indoor/outdoor swimming pool, spa and health club. Guests may spend their day bicycling, playing volleyball, basketball or tennis, boating, hiking with your dog, gaming at the casinos, relaxing on the private beach or participating in your favorite water sport when the weather permits. In the winter, you are just minutes away from several prime cross-country and downhill ski areas.

Holiday House

Holiday House
7276 N. Lake Boulevard
Tahoe Vista, CA 96148
800-294-6378
(916) 546-2369

Room Rates:	$85–$135
Pet Charges or Deposits:	$40 deposit
Rated: 3 Paws 🐾🐾🐾	7 lakefront rooms and suites with kitchenette, living room, separate bedroom, cable TV, barbecue and hot tub. Weekly rates available.

L ocated on the picturesque North Shore of Lake Tahoe, the Holiday House is set among tall pine trees. Here guests will find comfortable accommodations with extras like decks and kitchenettes.

In the summer, take advantage the waterfront locale by swimming, fishing, windsurfing, water skiing or rafting before heading into Tahoe for the nightlife. Winter promises just as much fun since you're only minutes from Northstar, Alpine Meadows, Incline and other ski resorts.

Cedar Stock Resort

Cedar Stock Resort
45810 State Highway 3
Trinity Center, CA 96091
800-982-2279
(916) 286-2225

Room Rates:	Cabins—$50 and up; Houseboats—$85 and up.
Pet Charges or Deposits:	$35 per pet
Rated: 3 Paws ❀❀❀	Cabins and houseboats, daily and weekly rentals, recreational and fishing boat rentals, boat marina with berth rentals, grocery store, restaurant and cocktail lounge.

L ocated on Trinity Lake, Cedar Stock Resort offers a choice of cabins or houseboats. The cabins have a private bath, fully equipped kitchen and barbecue. You bring the rest. When you don't feel like cooking, try the Cedar Stock Restaurant, a popular dinner house for the entire county. Top off the evening at The Lodge bar and lounge, where the whole family can relax with a cocktail or a soda. There is even a grocery store for supplies. Guests may rent horses, fishing and recreational boats, water and Jet Skis.

A great way to relax and explore Trinity Lake is by houseboat. Cedar Stock Resort rents five types of houseboats by the day or by the week. They come well-equipped. All you need to bring are linens, soaps, food, games and fishing gear. The rest you can buy at the resort's store.

Whichever accommodation you choose, with 500,000 acres of national parks surrounding the lake, your entire family, including your pets, are bound to have a great adventure.

Holiday Inn – Marine World Africa USA

Holiday Inn – Marine World Africa USA
1000 Fairgrounds Drive
Vallejo, CA 94589
800-HOLIDAY
(707) 644-1200

Room Rates:	$99–$150, AAA and AARP discounts.
Pet Charges or Deposits:	$25 charge
Rated: 3 Paws 🐾🐾🐾	166 rooms, located opposite the theme park, refrigerators, microwaves, courtyard pool and recreation area, game room, dry sauna, whirlpool, laundry facilities, meeting and banquet facilities, ballroom, restaurant and cocktail lounge, shuttle to San Francisco Airport.

Directly across the street from the Marine World Africa USA theme park and only 30 minutes from the San Francisco Bay Area is the Holiday Inn – Marine World Africa USA. Designed with comfort in mind, rooms are spacious and include a refrigerator and microwave, comfortable beds and a table and chairs perfect for finishing up that business report or enjoying your morning coffee.

Enjoy the moderate climate basking in the sun, refreshing in the pool or working out at the health club minutes from the hotel. Of course, don't forget the thrills and adventures that await across the street at Marine World Africa USA.

The hotel's Marine Grill Restaurant, adjacent to the lobby, offers American dining for breakfast, lunch or dinner. The Reef Lounge has daily specials, large-screen television and live entertainment and dancing on the weekends.

Embassy Suites Hotel

Embassy Suites Hotel
1345 Treat Boulevard
Walnut Creek, CA 94596
800-EMBASSY
(510) 934-2500

Room Rates: $119, AAA and AARP discounts.
Pet Charges or Deposits: $50 cleaning fee per pet.
Rated: 4 Paws 🐾🐾🐾🐾 249 suites with kitchen and living room, kitchen, dining/work area, mini-bar, refrigerator, microwave, atrium, meeting rooms, heated indoor pool, sauna, whirlpool, exercise room, library, game room, gift shop, restaurant and cocktail lounge.

In 1989, Walnut Creek, with its specialty shops, department stores, theaters, restaurants and the Regional Art Center was voted "Most livable small city in the nation" by the Conference of Mayors. The Walnut Creek – Embassy Suites Hotel is located within two miles of the charming downtown area.

Accommodations feature a large private bedroom, living room with a sofa bed, galley kitchen, mini-bar, refrigerator, microwave and a well-lighted dining/work area. Relax in the garden atrium or the outdoor sun deck with your complimentary morning paper, swim a few laps in the indoor pool or work out in the fitness center before heading out for a day of meetings or sightseeing. There is a shuttle service anywhere within a five-mile radius. Plus a nearby park allows for a quick romp with the dog.

When it comes to dining, the Taos Bar and Grill serves up Southwest cuisine with indoor or outdoor seating, or for a quick meal, stop by the Taos Deli that offers a more traditional American delicatessen.

Howard Creek Ranch

Howard Creek Ranch
40501 N. Highway 1
Westport, CA 95488
(707) 964-6725

Room Rates:	$55–$145, AAA, AARP and AKC and off-season discounts.
Pet Charges or Deposits:	None but manager's approval required; Pets allowed in designated rooms or cabins.
Rated: 3 Paws 🐾🐾🐾	7 rooms and suites, 3 cottages with handmade quilts, private decks or balconies, skylights, fireplaces or wood stoves, hot tub, sauna, microwave, refrigerator, gardens, horseback riding.

Howard Creek Ranch thrives in the rural splendor of sweeping mountain and ocean views on 40 acres near the "Lost Coast," a 60-mile-long wilderness area. Nestled on an oceanfront farm along the Mendocino Coast, the historic ranch was built in 1871. The New England-style farmhouse is bordered by miles of beach, mountains and open wilderness making this the perfect place to take your pet.

Accommodations include cabins, suites and rooms furnished with antiques, large comfortable beds and handmade quilts topped off with views of the ocean, mountains, creek or gardens.

Guests may relax in the hot tub, stroll the award-winning gardens, explore the 75-foot-long swinging footbridge over Howard Creek, spend the day horseback riding or combing the beach. The ranch is on the National Historic Register.

Golden Pheasant Inn – Best Western

Golden Pheasant Inn – Best Western
249 N. Humboldt Avenue
Willows, CA 95988
800-528-1234
(916) 934-4603

Room Rates:	$56–$150, AAA and AARP discounts.
Pet Charges or Deposits:	$10 per day
Rated: 3 Paws 🐾🐾🐾	104 garden guest rooms and suites, some with fireplace and Jacuzzi, landscaped grounds, 2 pools, laundry facilities, restaurant and tavern.

S urrounded by seven acres of landscaped gardens and lawns, the Golden Pheasant Inn – Best Western is a recently remodeled, full-service inn offering guests accommodations normally found in big city hotels yet set in a quiet, relaxing country environment at an affordable price.

At this oasis just off Interstate 5, weary travelers can enjoy the pool or spa or explore the local scenery and nearby wildlife refuge.

The inn restaurant and tavern offer guests American and Mexican cuisine in a newly renovated setting.

Vintage Inn – Napa Valley

Vintage Inn – Napa Valley
6541 Washington Street
Yountville, CA 94599
800-351-1133
(707) 944-1112

Room Rates:	$180–$325, AAA and AARP discounts.
Pet Charges or Deposits:	$25 per stay and credit card guarantee as deposit.
Rated: 4 Paws 🐾🐾🐾🐾	80 rooms with balcony or patio, views of the vineyard, mountain or town, fireplaces, refrigerators and whirlpool, nightly turndown, champagne breakfast, concierge, massage, air conditioning, conference facilities, landscaped grounds, heated lap pool, whirlpool spa, tennis courts, room service.

Nestled among the vineyards of the Napa Valley on lush, estate-like grounds is the country villa called the Vintage Inn. The Old World charm and contemporary amenities make this a popular choice for vacationers and business professionals.

After settling into your room with its custom furnishings, cozy fireplace and complimentary bottle of wine, stroll through the landscaped grounds and admire the pools, fountains and courtyards with your pet. For recreation, guests may play tennis, do a few laps in the heated pool, relax in the spa, treat themselves to a massage or visit the adjacent Vintage 1870, a restored winery with unique shops, restaurants and galleries.

Sheep Dung Estates

Sheep Dung Estates
P.O. Box 49
Yorkville, CA 95494
(707) 894-5322

Room Rates:	$75–$125
Pet Charges or Deposits:	None
Rated: 4 Paws 🐾🐾🐾🐾	3 cottages, with mini-kitchens, wood-burning fireplaces, private baths, set on several secluded acres.

Don't let the name fool you. Sheep Dung Estates is a unique country hideaway with grand views and meticulous attention to detail. Nestled on 160 acres of the picturesque Anderson Valley Hills, this retreat offers three secluded, comfortably furnished, modern cottages, with queen-sized beds, mini-kitchens and wood-burning fireplaces. The Pond Cottage, Sunset Hill and the Terra Cottage are each set 15-40 acres with views of the rolling hills.

Mini-kitchens come fully stocked with breakfast fixings. After a day of sightseeing and a trip to the vineyards or wandering rambling roads, you can prepare your evening feast, sit on your own private deck and toast the sun with a glass of local wine as it sets beyond the hills.

Northern California

Leashes are required unless otherwise stated.

ARCATA

Arcata Community Forest and Redwood Park is off of Samoa Boulevard at Union Street. Turn right onto 14th Street and continue through the forest to the parking area. Here you'll find 575 acres of lush forest. For more information, call (707) 822-7091.

Clam Beach County Park is 7 miles north of Arcata. Take the Clam Beach Park exit and head west for approximately 2 miles. Here your dog can run leash-free on the beach or play in the surf. For more information, call (707) 445-7652.

If you're looking for private, leash-free beaches, try Mad River County Park. It's a great place to bring a picnic and spend the day. Take the Guintoli Lane exit, turn right onto Heindon Road and follow the signs to the small parking lot at the end of the road. For more information, call (707) 445-7651.

BODEGA BAY

Doran Beach Regional Park, off of Highway 1 on Doran Park Road, requires leashes but is a great place to take a brisk hike or a refreshing swim. For more information, call (707) 875-3540.

CHICO

Bidwell Park is a 2,250-acre city park stretching from the downtown area to the foothills of the Sierra Nevada. Here you have your choice of hiking and bicycling trails, a playground for the kids, ball fields, swimming, golf or horseshoes. For more information, call (916) 891-5556.

EUREKA

Samoa Dunes Recreation Area has 300 acres of leash-free coastal dunes. If you and your pet love the water, this is a great place to hike or take a dip in the ocean. Take Highway 255 to the Samoa Peninsula, turn left on New Navy Base Road for about 5 miles. There is a main lot for parking. For more information, call (707) 825-2300.

FREMONT

Ardenwood Historic Farm is on Ardenwood Boulevard, 25 miles north of Highway 84. The farm is a living history project showing farm life from the 1870s to the 1920s. The grounds of the George Washington Patterson's Victorian mansion are covered in beautiful gardens. Here you may purchase fresh picked vegetables, visit the period shops, picnic or visit resident farm animals. There is an entrance fee and a separate fee for tours of the mansion. For more information, call (510) 769-0663.

Coyote Hills Regional Park is west on Highway 84 then exit at Thornton Avenue-Paseo Padre Parkway. Head north 1 mile and the park is at 8000 Patterson Ranch Road. Here you will find a 976-acre wildlife refuge for white-tailed kites and red-tailed hawks. There are 2,400-year-old Indian shell mounds, a reconstructed Indian village, a freshwater marsh, picnic facilities and more than 40 miles of hiking, bicycling and jogging trails. While you are there, stop by the visitors center and the museum. There is a day-use fee and a fee for your dog. For more information, call (510) 795-9385.

Fremont Central Park is a waterfowl refuge and lake with jogging and bicycling trails plus a variety of boats for rent. The scenery is beautiful, on or off the water, and it is a wonderful place for a picnic or day on the lake. There is no entrance fee, but there is a swimming fee. The park is on Paseo Padre Parkway and Stevenson Boulevard. For more information, call (510) 791-4340.

Mission Peak Regional Preserve is 3,000 acres of spacious grasslands. There are plenty of trails to explore and wonderful views stretching from Mount Tamalpais to Mount Hamilton. Heading east, take Mission Boulevard to Stanford Avenue, turn right and head about one mile to the entrance. For more information, call (510) 635-0135.

Sunol Regional Wilderness offers hours of geological wonders and lots of scenic trails. Make sure to visit the whirlpools and waterfalls at Alameda Creek. To reach the park, go north on Interstate 680 and exit on Calaveras Road in Sunol. Turn right on Calaveras to Geary Road, then left into the park. For more information, call (510) 635-0135.

GLEN ELLEN

Jack London State Historic Park, 1 mile west on Jack London Ranch Road, offers visitors and leashed dogs 800 acres for picnicking, hiking, biking or horseback riding. Home and resting place of the famed author, his ranch house contains his personal papers, belongings and mementos. The park is open daily with guided tours offered on weekends. For more information, call (707) 938-5216.

GRAEAGLE – BLAIRSDEN

Plumas National Forest is 1,162,863 acres of wilderness straddling the Sierra Nevada and the Cascades Mountains. Here you will find forest lands and wonderful scenery where you can go camping, hiking, boating, fishing, swimming or rent horses and bicycles. The Feather River has carved several canyons and ravines full of white water and cascades. There is a 15,000-acre scenic area with the 640-foot Feather Falls above Lake Oroville. You can hike and camp along the river, but due to the rugged terrain and rapids, be sure to stick to the recreational zones for water sports. There are several entrances into the park. Contact Plumas National Forest for directions and further information at (916) 283-2050.

INVERNESS

Rocky cliffs rise from the sea at Point Reyes National Seashore. Here you and your dog can roam the beaches, but leashes are required. Take Bear Valley Road off of Highway 1. For more information, call (415) 663-1092.

Kehoe Beach is a half-mile hike from the road through wildflower fields. Here the whitecapped waves crash against the limestone cliffs forming tide pools. Leashes are required, but there is plenty of beach to comb. You'll enjoy watching the harbor seals and snowy plovers that have made this area their home. For more information, call (415) 663-1092.

Tomales Point, with its bluffs and moors, can be a temperamental place. The 4.7 miles of one-way hiking above the ocean is a favorite of many hikers. The mist and vapors from the sea will keep you cool as you hike the trail. Leashes are required, but it's a fine trail.

MENDOCINO

Jackson Demonstration State Forest has 50,000 acres of trees, trails and logging roads for you and your pooch to explore. It is 9 miles west of Willits, off Highway 20, east of Mendocino and Fort Bragg. For more information, call (707) 964-5674.

Mendocino Headlands State Park/Big River Beach requires leashes, but it's worth it to experience the spectacular scenery. Located off Highway 1 south; exit at the Mendocino Headlands State Park/Big River Beach sign. For more information, call (707) 964-5474.

Mendocino National Forest is 886,048 acres in the North Coast Mountain Range north of San Francisco. In addition to numerous scenic points, the park offers camping, picnicking, hiking, hang gliding, motorcycling areas, boating, boat rentals, fishing and swimming. Forest supervisor is at 420 E. Laurel Street, Willows, CA 95988. For more information, call (916) 934-2350.

MOUNT SHASTA

The Ellen Rupp Nature Study Area, situated among a pine forest, is the perfect place for you and your dog to study native plants along the half-mile trail before dipping your paws into a crystal clear stream. For more information, call (916) 926-4865.

Glass Mountain, off Highway 89 on Forest Service Road 43N99 on the southern edge of the mountain, is an intriguing place for geological hobbyists. An actual glass mountain caused by a volcanic vent, this rare geological phenomenon has a glass flow that spans 4,210 acres. For more information, call (916) 964-2184.

Medicine Lake Loop Trail is off Highway 89, near Bartle. Take Forest Service Road 49 to Medicine Lake Road. Once the center of an active volcano, the clear lake is stocked with 30,000 brook trout yearly, offering visitors a chance to do some shore fishing. There are also ice caves for you and your dog to explore before heading to the smaller lakes in the area. For more information, call (916) 964-2184.

NORTH SHORE TAHOE

North Tahoe Regional Park is in Tahoe Vista at Donner Road and National Avenue off of Highway 28. Leashes are required, but the 108 acres and 4 miles of hiking trails eventually run into the Tahoe National Forest, which is leash-free. For more information, call (916) 546-7248.

Tahoe National Forest has 797,205 acres that are part of the Lake Tahoe Basin. Leashes are required, but there are plenty of hiking trails and room to roam as well as activities galore from which to choose, including camping, boating, horseback riding, fishing and swimming. For more information, call (916) 265-4531.

RANCHO CORDOVA

Folsom Lake State Recreation Area is off of Highway 50. Exit at Folsom and continue north to Folsom Auburn Road. Here you'll find plenty of wildlife, scenery and 80 miles of hiking trails. There is a day-use fee for the park and a small fee for the dog. For more information, call (800) 444-7275.

ROHNERT PARK

Crane Creek Regional Park is east of town on Pressley Road off of Roberts Road, then 2 miles east of Petaluma Hill Road. Here you will find oak and maple trees beside picturesque creekside trails plus 128 acres to explore. For more information, call (707) 527-2041.

SACRAMENTO

American River Parkway, off Interstate 5 at Richards Boulevard; exit to Jibboom Street. Trails lead you along the American River, stretching from Discovery Park in Sacramento to Folsom. With no leash laws, you and your pet can take full advantage of the bike and equestrian trails. For more information, call (916) 366-2061.

Loch Leven Lake, a leash-free haven off Interstate 80 at the Big Bend exit, has everything from alpine meadows, grassy valleys, granite cliffs, towering woodlands and three beautiful lakes. The paths take you over the railroad tracks, across a creek and through the forest. You'll want to spend an entire day in this splendid place. For more information, call (916) 265-4531.

ST. HELENA

Bothe-Napa Valley State Park consists of 1,916 acres of meadows full of wildflowers in the spring and plenty of trails for hiking and biking, plus lots of wilderness to explore. Located 3 miles northwest on State Route 29, near Bale Grist Mill State Historic Park, a restored flour mill. There are hiking trails that lead across the mill pond to Bothe-Napa Valley State Park. You may rent horses for a trail ride, go camping, picnicking, swimming or take a nature tour of the area. There is a small gate fee. Stop by the visitors center for information on the park.

SAN FRANCISCO

Golden Gate Park requires leashes, but with 1,000 acres to explore, it won't slow you and your dog down. The park is bordered by Fulton, Lincoln and Stanyan streets and the Great Highway. There are leash-free areas within the park. You'll both enjoy the miles of bridle and foot paths that make this the perfect place to go hiking, play catch or have a picnic with your favorite canine.

Golden Gate National Recreation Area encompasses both the rolling coastal hills and diverse urban park lands. Wrapping around San Francisco's northern and western edges and extending to San Mateo County, this national recreation area offers a leashless adventure for you and your dog. From the windswept sands of Ocean Beach to the Victorian Gardens of Sutro Heights and Lands End, the coastal trails thread through to China and Baker beaches.

The Golden Gate Promenade extends 3.5 miles along San Francisco Bay and connects Fort Point with Crissy Field and Fort Mason. The park is at the south end of the Golden Gate Bridge. Exit at Marina Boulevard and go southwest toward Fisherman's Wharf. The area from Marina Green to the west gate of Crissy Field is leash-free, making this a tail-wagging experience. The information center is at the Fort Mason headquarters. For more information, call (415) 556-0560.

SAN MATEO

Laurelwood Park, at Glendora and Cedarwood drives, is a tree-laden paradise for your dog. Here you can spend the day hiking along the stream and enjoy the great outdoors with your dog.

SAN RAMON

Bishop Ranch Regional Open Space is a wonderfully serene park that is a haven for red-tailed hawks, turkey vultures and deer. The park is off of Bolinger Canyon Road and San Ramon Valley Boulevard on Morgan Drive. For more information, call (510) 562-7275.

TRINITY CENTER

Trinity Lake is east of Highway 3. Here you can rent a boat and spend the day sailing, fishing or pack a picnic lunch and spend the day lazing on shore with your dog. For more information, call (916) 623-6101.

WALNUT CREEK

Las Trampas Regional Wilderness Park is 3,600 acres of predominantly leash-free paradise for you and your dog. With acre after acre of wooded canyons, scenic wilderness, abundant hiking trails and spectacular views, you will want to spend the entire day exploring this untamed world off of Highway 24. Take the Pleasant Hill exit south and turn right on Olympic Boulevard; then head for the Olympic Staging Area. For more information, call (510) 635-0135.

Mount Diablo State Park is a 3,849-foot summit overlooking 35 counties, 17 miles southeast on Diablo Road. This 18,000-acre park offers horse rentals, camping, picnicking, hiking and bicycle trails and a visitors center with nature study programs. For more information, call (510) 635-0135.

WESTPORT

Westport Union Landing State Beach is on Highway 1 north. This isolated beach is great for a relaxing picnic. For more information, call (707) 937-5804.

WILLOWS

Sacramento National Wildlife Refuge requires leashes. There are 10,783 acres of marshland that is home to migrating birds and a wide variety of wildlife. Located off Route 57. After exiting, go approximately 6 miles on the frontage road to the entrance. For more information, call (916) 934-2801.

Central California

Apple Lane Inn

Apple Lane Inn Bed and Breakfast
6265 Soquel Drive
Aptos, CA 95003
800-649-8988
(408) 475-6868

Room Rates:	$95–$150, including breakfast. AAA, AARP and AKC discounts.
Pet Charges or Deposits:	$25 fee plus $250 refundable deposit or credit card imprint. Horses welcome.
Rated: 4 Paws 🐾🐾🐾🐾	5 rooms with private baths, some sitting rooms and meadow views.

O ne of Santa Cruz County's oldest farmhouses is also among its first bed and breakfast inns. The Apple Lane Inn is a charming Victorian house and barn, lovingly restored to reflect the original 1872 character and set on three acres amid fields and apple orchards.

Guests may choose from 5 private rooms with romantic decor, antique furniture, plump quilts and picturesque views of the meadows. Before heading out for a day of beachcombing and sightseeing with your four-legged friend, begin your day with an elegant country breakfast of fresh fruit, juice, pastries, a hearty main course and special coffee blends.

If you prefer to linger at the historical inn, owners Doug and Diana Groom invite you to unwind in the front parlor with a glass of wine or a book; play darts, cards, horseshoes or croquet; visit resident animals in the barn; pick apples from the orchard; or relax in the white, Victorian gazebo surrounded by the trim lawn, flowering gardens and wisteria arbors, a popular place for weddings and special gatherings.

Carmel Country Inn

Carmel Country Inn
Third and Dolores
Carmel, CA 93921
800-215-6343
(408) 625-3263

Room Rates:	$95–$135, AAA, AARP and AKC discounts.
Pet Charges or Deposits:	$10 per day plus nightly room rate as deposit.
Rated: 4 Paws 🐾🐾🐾🐾	12 rooms, including suites and studios, some with fireplaces, near local attractions.

You'll remember the flowers at the Carmel Country Inn, both those in the colorful gardens and the freshly cut ones placed in your room. Serving up a blend of comfort, convenience, romance and natural beauty, the inn is nestled in a quiet, residential area within three blocks of the center of quaint Carmel.

Secluded in its lovely garden setting, the inn (formerly the Dolores Lodge) offers large one- and two-bedroom suites, with comfortable sitting rooms and fireplaces. Start your day off with a continental breakfast in the cheerful country kitchen before heading out to explore the village's shops, galleries and restaurants. The residential neighborhood, parks and beaches are all inviting experiences for you and your pet in this animal-friendly community.

Carmel Mission Inn Best Western

Carmel Mission Inn Best Western
3665 Rio Road
Carmel, California 93923
800-348-9090
(408) 624-1841

Room Rates:	$79–$149, AAA and AARP discounts.
Pet Charges or Deposits:	$25; manager's approval required.
Rated: 3 Paws 🐾🐾🐾	165 newly remodeled rooms and suites with terraces and guest rooms, full-service restaurant, room service, secretarial services, bicycle rentals, minutes from shopping, beaches and local attractions.

Perched at the mouth of pastoral Carmel Valley, within a private garden setting, is the Carmel Mission Inn Best Western. Here guests will find the amenities and meeting facilities of a large hotel wrapped in the intimacy and warmth of a country inn.

The historic Carmel Mission is a must-see, especially when it's only steps away. While the inn is mere minutes from downtown Carmel's shops, art galleries, restaurants and pristine beaches, the surrounding neighborhood offers plenty of opportunities, too, for a stroll through adjacent shops and restaurants in The Barnyard and The Crossroads shopping areas. If you prefer to dine in, Sassy's Bar and Grill boasts a varied menu and cocktail lounge.

To keep pets engaged during your stay, the inn offers a choice of dog runs, exercise areas and a pet playground. And remember, Carmel Beach at the end of Ocean Avenue allows supervised dogs to run free.

Cypress Inn

Cypress Inn
Lincoln and Seventh Streets
Carmel, CA 93921
800-443-7443
(408) 624-3871

Room Rates:	$95–$145, including continental breakfast
Pet Charges or Deposits:	$17 per day and first night's room payment in advance; pet sitters available.
Rated: 4 Paws 🐾🐾🐾🐾	33 stately rooms, sitting rooms, verandas or ocean views, garden courtyard.

S ince fellow animal lover Doris Day is one of its owners, it's of little surprise that the historic Cypress Inn is open to pets. Built in 1929 in the heart of Carmel-by-the-Sea, the 33-room inn is known for its classic, stately interior and brilliant white Mediterranean exterior, with Spanish tiled roof and intimate garden courtyard.

Each room is distinct in its character and charm, offering a choice of sitting rooms, verandas or ocean views. While the accommodations may vary, the staff's warmth and personal attention to detail is constant here. Guests awake to a generous continental breakfast served in the warmth of the sunny breakfast room or in the serenity of the garden courtyard. In the evening, relax in the elegant "living room" lobby with its overstuffed sofas, soft music and cozy fire.

Forest Lodge and Suites

Forest Lodge and Suites
Ocean Avenue and Torres Street
Carmel, CA 93921
(408) 624-7023

Room Rates: $149–$240, including breakfast. Call for discounts.
Pet Charges or Deposits: $5 to $10 per stay
Rated: 3 Paws 🐾🐾🐾   1 deluxe room in the main house, plus 3 cottages with
                                  fireplaces and full baths, 1 includes full kitchen, garden setting,
                                  near town and beach.

T ucked away in the quaint village of Carmel is the charming Forest Lodge and Suites, built in the early 1920s by a Dutch immigrant and horticulturist, Johan Hagemeyer. Two of the spaces, the Garret and the Manor House, were later set up as a studio and a workshop for his photography. His subjects included such famous visitors to Carmel as Salvador Dali and Albert Einstein.

Majestic oak trees and lush, flowering English gardens surround these unique accommodations. The Garret is a spacious loft in the main house featuring a king-size bed and fireplace. The Cottage-in-the-Glen offers a queen bed and fireplace while the Garden House has two queen-size beds and fireplace. The Manor House features a full kitchen, fireplace and two queen-size beds.

Spend the day exploring the many shops, galleries and restaurants in the village. And don't forget to head down to leash-free Carmel Beach with your dog for an oceanfront romp.

Lincoln Green Inn

Lincoln Green Inn
Carmelo between 15th and 16th Streets
Carmel, CA 93921
800-262-1262
(408) 624-1880

Room Rates:	$165–$205
Pet Charges or Deposits:	$10 per day; manager's approval required.
Rated: 4 Paws 😻😻😻😻	4 separate cottages with kitchens, full baths, large living areas and ocean views.

Ensconced on picturesque Carmel Point, a mere stone's throw from River Beach, is the Lincoln Green Inn. As you enter the English country garden setting of this romantic, Shakespearean-style inn, you'll discover four steep-peaked, white English cottages with forest green shutters. Each cottage has cathedral ceilings, a large living area and bedroom, Carmel stone fireplace, kitchen, full bath and ocean views.

Relax on the sun deck and drink in the scenic view of the Big Sur Mountains and Carmel Point, or stroll through the wild bird reserve and lagoon adjacent to the property. Take advantage of the no-leash law on Carmel Beach for a picnic or an afternoon walk on the sandy shores with your dog.

The Quail Lodge

The Quail Lodge
8205 Valley Greens Drive
Carmel, CA 92923
800-538-9516
(408) 624-1581

Room Rates:	$215 and up
Pet Charges or Deposits:	None; in designated rooms only; dogs only.
Rated: 5 Paws 🐾🐾🐾🐾🐾	100 luxury rooms, suites and cottages; conference and banquet facilities; 18-hole golf course and four tennis courts with professional golf and tennis instructors; two pools; croquet court; hot tub; sauna; jogging, hiking and bicycling paths; picnic areas; bicycle rentals.

S et in the sunny part of Carmel among lush fairways, oak-studded meadows, rolling hills and sparkling lakes, the Quail Lodge Resort and Golf Club combines natural beauty with five-star resort elegance. From private decks and patios, each room overlooks either the lakes, the golf course or lush gardens.

Recreational pursuits include golf on the championship course, tennis, swimming, jogging or hiking with your dog. Or spend your day exploring the many shops and galleries in the quaint village of Carmel-by-the-Sea.

Start the day with breakfast at the Country Club dining room, with its scenic views of the resort. For evening dining, the recently renovated and award-winning Covey Restaurant has unveiled a new menu based on the abundance of fresh ingredients found on the Central Coast. With views of the lake with its arched foot bridge and lighted fountain, as well as live entertainment Wednesday through Sunday, it's a comfortable place to sit back and enjoy refreshments and the view.

Sunset House Bed and Breakfast

Sunset House Bed and Breakfast
Camino Real between Ocean and Seventh Avenues
Carmel, CA 93921
(408) 624-4884

Room Rates:	$150–$190, including breakfast.
Pet Charges or Deposits:	$20 cleaning fee; small dogs only.
Rated: 3 Paws 🐾 🐾 🐾	5 rooms with fireplaces, some with sitting areas, ocean views, canopy beds and kitchenettes; close to town and beach.

Located only a few blocks from Carmel Beach, in the heart of Carmel, this romantic inn captures the essence of this quaint town. Guests may choose from five cottage-style rooms, with their antique decor and charm and wood-burning fireplaces.

The South Room offers tree-top views with a glimpse of the blue Pacific. For privacy, try the West Room and its cathedral-beamed ceiling. The North Room offers a king size "Hans Christian Anderson" bed, cozy sitting area and ocean view. For a tree-top getaway, with ocean views, outside deck and kitchenette, choose the Hideaway Room. Finally, there is the romantic canopy bed and Jacuzzi tub in the Patio Room.

No matter which accommodation you choose, you'll enjoy the uniquely decorated rooms, private baths and the pampering touch of a breakfast tray brought to your room each morning.

Vagabond's House Inn

Vagabond's House Inn
Fourth Avenue and Dolores Street
Carmel, CA 92921
800-262-1262
(408) 624-7738

Room Rates: $85–$165, including continental breakfast.
Rated: 4 Paws 🐾🐾🐾🐾   11 rooms with fireplaces, some kitchens and courtyard.

Nestled in the heart of Carmel is the Vagabond's House, a charming brick and half-timbered English Tudor country inn. Your experience begins as you enter the delightful courtyard with its ancient oak tree, cascading waterfall, hanging plants, Camellias, rhododendrons, ferns and flowers creating an almost magical atmosphere.

This is an ideal spot to daydream or relax with an intriguing book and a glass of local wine. Accommodations include guest rooms with fireplaces and traditional country decor. The guest parlor offers a variety of collections, including toys and books from the '20s, '30s and '40s. The charming courtyard is the setting for your continental breakfast, or you may have it served in your room. Then put on your walking shoes, grab the dog's leash and head out for a day of exploring the village.

Wayside Inn

Wayside Inn
Seventh and Mission
Carmel, CA 93921
800-433-4732
(408) 624-5336

Room Rates:	$99–$249, including continental breakfast. AAA and AARP discounts.
Pet Charges or Deposits:	First night room rate in advance.
Rated: 3 Paws 🐾🐾🐾	22 rooms and suites, some with wood-burning fireplaces and kitchens.

Conveniently set in the heart of downtown Carmel is the charming, Colonial Williamsburg-style Wayside Inn. Accommodations include homey furnishings, wood-paneled walls, spacious rooms and suites big enough for the entire family, including your pets. Many rooms include a wood-burning fireplace and a full kitchen.

The inn kicks off your day with a complimentary continental breakfast and newspaper delivered to your door each morning. After you have enjoyed your breakfast, take a walk around the artistic village or head to the beach with your dog where he can run free along the sandy shoreline.

Valley Lodge

Valley Lodge
Carmel Valley and Ford Roads
Carmel Valley, CA 93924
800-641-4646
(408) 659-2261

Room Rates:	$99–$337, including a generous continental breakfast, AAA and AARP discounts.
Pet Charges or Deposits:	$10 per day and room rate as a deposit.
Rated: 4 Paws 🐾🐾🐾🐾	31 guest rooms and studios and 8 cottages with fireplace and kitchen, antique furnishings, meeting rooms, pool, sauna, whirlpool, exercise room and landscaped grounds.

When looking for a lush and relaxing setting in the sun belt of the Monterey Peninsula, the Valley Lodge has plenty to offer. Tucked into the rolling hills of the sunny Carmel Valley, this quiet country inn makes a peaceful retreat for guests wishing to escape crowds. Choose from a garden patio room, fireplace studios or individual one- and two-bedroom fireplace cottages, individually decorated with classic Shaker furniture and quilted bed spreads, with open beamed ceilings and modern conveniences. The cottages offer the added bonus of wood-burning stoves and kitchens with microwaves.

Start each morning with fresh brewed coffee and a generous continental breakfast before heading out to explore the shops in Carmel Valley Village or wandering through the shops and galleries of Carmel. If you are feeling adventurous, you can hike through the hills with your dog, play golf or tennis, swim, ride horses or relax in the lush garden setting. The resident lodge dog, "Lucky," will gladly show you around.

Harris Ranch Inn and Restaurants

Harris Ranch Inn and Restaurants
I-5 and Highway 19
Coalinga, CA 93210
800-942-2333
(209) 935-0717

Room Rates:	$89–$225, AAA and AARP discounts.
Pet Charges or Deposits:	$10 per day; manager's approval required.
Rated: 5 Paws 🐾🐾🐾🐾🐾	123 rooms and 28 suites, Olympic-style pool, Jacuzzis, fitness facility, conference and party rooms, grand ballroom, private airstrip, country store, restaurants, bar and lounge.

Built in 1937, the Harris Ranch Inn exudes early California charm and family hospitality. Guests may choose from 123 deluxe rooms and 28 luxury suites with a patio or balcony, overlooking the courtyard, the pool or a view of the ranch lands.

The hacienda setting beckons travelers to lounge in the courtyard by the pool, relax in the spa, work out at the fitness center or explore the spacious, landscaped grounds with your four-legged friend.

When it comes to tempting dining, guests may opt for the Ranch Kitchen, featuring the ranch's renowned beef and ranch-style meals. The Jockey Club, with a decor that pays tribute to the ranch's equestrian history and award-winning thoroughbreds, serves up beef specialties and other country favorites. Guests may also take a lunch or dinner break in The Bar and Lounge's western atmosphere.

Tenaya Lodge at Yosemite

Tenaya Lodge at Yosemite
1122 Highway 41
Fish Camp, CA 93623
800-635-5807
(209) 683-6555

Room Rates:	$89–$259, AAA and AARP discounts.
Pet Charges or Deposits:	$50 cleaning fee.
Rated: 4 Paws 🐾🐾🐾🐾	242 non-smoking rooms and suites, some sunken tubs and wet bars, indoor and outdoor pools, sauna, steam room, whirlpool, data ports, conference and banquet facilities, laundry facilities, restaurant, coffee shop and cocktail lounge.

Yosemite's natural splendor has inspired the photographs of Ansel Adams and the writings of John Muir as well as captivated millions of visitors. Just two miles from the national park's south entrance, visitors to the area will find the Tenaya Lodge.

Surrounded by acres of Sierra National Forest, this smoke-free resort invites guests to escape the hustle and bustle of the outside world. Spend the day exploring the natural wonders of the area with your pet, before escaping to the spa to relieve stress with a relaxing massage. With three restaurants on premises, guests may enjoy informal snacks or fine dining. They'll even pack a picnic for your to savor al fresco on a hike through the redwoods. The Guest Experience Center will arrange outings, too, from mountain biking to a ride on a steam-driven logging train.

For business and executive needs, the lodge boasts 7,500 square feet of conference and banquet facilities.

Fresno Garden Court Inn – Best Western

Fresno Garden Court Inn – Best Western
2141 North Parkway Drive
Fresno, CA 93705
800-4-FRESNO
(209)-237-1881

Room Rates:	$48–$62, AAA, AARP, AKC and ABA discounts.
Pet Charges or Deposits:	$5 per day; pets up to 40 pounds.
Rated: 3 Paws 🐾🐾🐾	108 spacious rooms with coffee makers, microwaves and refrigerators, some with garden view, spacious landscaped courtyard, meeting rooms, pool and whirlpool, dog runs.

Set on 10 lusciously landscaped acres in the heart of the Central Valley is the charming Garden Court Inn – Best Western. Here travelers will find spacious accommodations overlooking the garden courtyard, with four acres of undeveloped land adjacent to the inn.

Spend part of the day relaxing in the outdoor spa or swimming pool. If land games are more your style, try your hand at shuffleboard or take the dog for a quick jog around the grounds. Be sure to ask desk personnel to direct you to the Chaffee Zoological Gardens in Roeding Park within walking distance to the inn.

For dining, the Gaslight Steakhouse serves up prime rib, charcoal-broiled steaks, seafood, fresh-baked breads and tantalizing desserts. Try the full-service coffee shop for a more casual meal anytime of the day.

The Groveland Hotel

The Groveland Hotel
18767 Main Street
Groveland, CA 95321
800-273-3314
(209) 962-4000

Room Rates:	$95–$175
Pet Charges or Deposits:	$10 per day; manager's approval required.
Rated: 3 Paws 🐾🐾🐾	18-room bed and breakfast hotel, all rooms with private baths, European antiques, down comforters, getaway packages available.

Founded in 1849, the Groveland Hotel was once part of a thriving gold mining town. Today the original adobe hotel has been combined with an adjacent Queen Anne-style hostelry, originally built in 1914 to house VIP guests. The elegant, 18-room bed and breakfast hotel has recently undergone a million-dollar renovation, yet has retained its 19th-century character insuring travelers a look into the past while still enjoying modern comforts.

Groveland offers guests and their pets the luxury of wide open spaces. Go fishing, hiking, try white-water rafting on the Tuolumne River, visit the nearby Gold Rush towns or explore the natural bounty of Yosemite National Park. After a day of adventure in this slice of small-town California amidst the spectacular scenery of the Sierra Nevada, relax in the courtyard with a glass of spirits from the saloon before sampling the hotel restaurant's seasonal cuisine.

Zaballa House Bed and Breakfast

Zaballa House Bed and Breakfast
324 Main Street
Half Moon Bay, CA 94019
(415) 726-9123

Room Rates:	$75–$250, including full breakfast.
Pet Charges or Deposits:	$10 per stay
Rated: 3 Paws 🐾🐾🐾	12 guest rooms with private baths, some with whirlpool tubs and fireplaces.

O n historic Main Street, within walking distance to shops and restaurants, stands the historic Zaballa House. Built in 1859, it is the oldest building in Half Moon Bay.

This friendly, 12-room inn offers guests a casual, homey atmosphere. Put your feet up and relax in front of the fire with a book or magazine in the parlor or enjoy the privacy of your room, decorated with antiques, original oil paintings and wallpaper. All rooms offer private baths, some with double-sized whirlpool tubs, and fireplaces.

Sample the large breakfast menu before heading out for a day of beachcombing or hiking with your dog, or go bicycling, horseback riding, shopping or sightseeing. In the evening, you're invited to relax and socialize with the other guests with complimentary beverages and hors d'oeuvres in the front parlor.

Madera Valley Inn – Best Western

Madera Valley Inn – Best Western
317 North G Street
Madera, CA 93637
(209) 673-5164

Room Rates:	$56–$87, AAA, AARP, AKC and ABA discounts.
Pet Charges or Deposits:	None
Rated: 3 Paws 🐾🐾🐾	95 rooms and suites, some with refrigerators, secluded heated pool, laundry service, coffee shop and cocktail lounge.

Madera Valley Inn – Best Western is set in the nation's fruit bowl, just minutes from Yosemite National Park, King's Canyon and Sequoia National Park. Guests will appreciate spacious rooms and the convenience of the coffee shop, open for any meal of the day. Vacationers heading to the lake with boats and trailers will find ample parking here.

Since the inn is near the western Sierra Nevada Mountains, it's a convenient winter destination with access ski areas. In the spring and summer, the allure is fishing, boating, water skiing, hiking or exploring nearby Yosemite, King's Canyon and Sequoia parks, where you and your dog can enjoy nature at its best.

Sequoia Inn – Best Western

Sequoia Inn – Best Western
1213 V Street
Merced, CA 95340
800-735-3711
(209) 723-3711

Room Rates:	$49–$69, AAA and AARP discounts.
Pet Charges or Deposits:	$10 deposit
Rated: 3 Paws 🐾🐾🐾	97 remodeled rooms, heated pool, cable and color TV, free HBO, 80 miles to Yosemite National Park.

A Central Valley landmark and favorite resting stop for travelers heading to Yosemite National Park, the Sequoia Inn offers visitors comfortable accommodations with a selection of guest room amenities such as complimentary coffee, microwaves, refrigerators and free in-room movies. Business travelers will be pleased with the moderate rates, convenient meeting and conference facilities. The restaurant and lounge offer California cuisine in a comfortable, pleasant surrounding. Pets and children stay free.

Bay Park Hotel

Bay Park Hotel
1425 Munras Avenue
Monterey, CA 93940
800-338-3564
(408) 649-1020

Room Rates:	$76–$160, AAA and AARP discounts.
Pet Charges or Deposits:	$5 per day
Rated: 3 Paws 🐾🐾🐾	80 rooms, meeting rooms, pool and restaurant, near shopping and local attractions.

Set among the Monterey pines at the crest of Carmel hill, Bay Park Hotel stands midway between the quaint charm of Carmel-by-the-Sea and the history of Monterey, affording views of the bay and wooded hillside. The rustic allure of its natural wood decor comes packaged with modern amenities such as remote-control TV, air conditioning, clock radios and morning coffee.

Priding itself as a "family style" operation, the hotel is across the street from a city park for you and your pet to enjoy as well as the Del Monte Shopping Center for an afternoon of shopping. For relaxing after a day of local adventures, guests have the option of a bricked spa, full-size pool, a gazebo and the hotel's Crazy Horse Restaurant and Bar.

Monterey Beach Hotel

Monterey Beach Hotel
2600 Sand Dunes Drive
Monterey, CA 93940
800-242-8627
(408) 394-3321

Room Rates:	$89–$199, AAA and AARP discounts.
Pet Charges or Deposits:	$25 per stay
Rated: 3 Paws 🐾🐾🐾	196 large rooms, ocean views, conference and meeting facilities, pool, whirlpool, restaurant and cocktail lounge.

T he Monterey Beach Hotel is the area's only beachfront hotel. As such its affords guests miles of California's most scenic views with white dunes and sandy beaches encircling the Monterey Bay.

Many rooms come equipped with microwaves and refrigerators for in-room snacks or enjoy a meal anytime of the day or night from the hotel's restaurant perched on the top floor with a grand view. The new lounge on the main floor invites guests to enjoy afternoon hors d'oeuvres and spirits while watching a colorful sunset.

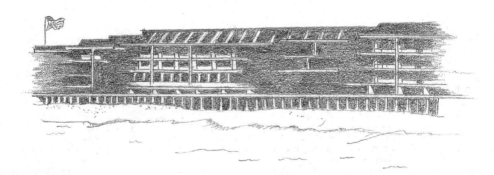

Victorian Inn

Victorian Inn
487 Foam Street
Monterey, CA 93940
800-232-4141
(408) 373-1602

Room Rates:	$179–$339, AAA, AARP and AKC discounts.
Pet Charges or Deposits:	$100 deposit; $75 refundable
Rated: 3 Paws ❧ ❧ ❧	68 rooms with fireplaces, private patios, balconies or window seats; hot tub, walking distance to local attractions, "Pooch Package" given upon check-in.

L ocated on Monterey's historic Cannery Row, the Victorian Inn combines the best of old and new in what it calls "an oasis of tranquillity." Guests step into hospitality and classic luxury upon entering any of the 68 guest rooms, which include a marble fireplace and honor bar, with either a private patio, balcony or window seat.

To make guests feel welcome, the inn plays host to an afternoon wine and cheese reception in the parlor, a lavish continental breakfast and, for the canine guests, presents a "Pooch Package" containing a bowl with the inn's logo filled with dog cookies, bottled water and a postcard for Fido to send to a friend back home.

Andril Fireplace Cottages

Andril Fireplace Cottages
569 Asilomar
Pacific Grove, CA 93950
(408) 375-0994

Room Rates:	$70–$285
Pet Charges or Deposits:	$8 per day.
Rated: 3 Paws 🐾🐾🐾	16 cottages with separated living areas, kitchens, fireplaces, some with decks or yards, and a 5 bedroom ranch house all in a private setting near the beach.

L ocated on a quiet corner in a residential area near the beautiful Pacific Ocean is the charming Andril Fireplace Cottages. This relaxing hideaway consists of sixteen separate cottages set among the pine trees within walking distance to Asilomar State Beach. Each cottage offers a wood burning fireplace, homey, comfortable furnishings, a fully equipped kitchen, color television with cable, and a private telephone.

For your recreational pleasure there is ping pong, a spa, and barbecues. Take advantage of your location for a leisurely stroll along the beach with your dog, explore the numerous tidepools, or merely take a few moments to enjoy the breathtaking sunset. Everything is within easy reach of your accommodations. After your day sightseeing and visiting all the local shops and galleries, you will appreciate the comfortable, homey feeling of a cozy fire in your private cottage.

EdgeWater Inn

EdgeWater Inn
1977 West Manning Avenue
Reedley, CA 93654
800-479-5855
(209) 637-7777

Room Rates:	$49–$125, AAA and AARP discounts.
Pet Charges or Deposits:	$7 per day; small pets only.
Rated: 3 Paws 🐾🐾🐾	50 rooms and master suites, heated pool, whirlpool, air conditioning and some refrigerators. Close to national parks and lakes.

Fresno County's Blossom Trail is a 63-mile self-guided driving tour showcasing the beauty of California's wildflowers and agriculture. Located on the Blossom Trail, a mere 500 feet from the sparkling Kings River, the EdgeWater Inn offers guests comfort and convenience framed in scenic surroundings.

You and your travel companion, human or canine, may laze next to the river under large trees or partake of this Sierra river's different personalities with white-water rafting or a quiet canoe tour. The inn boasts a large swimming pool and spa, and for the younger set, there is an adjacent toddler's lot. Large master suites provide home-like amenities, including a spacious living room and dining room, as well as a microwave and refrigerator.

This little river town, dubbed "The World's Fruit Basket," also features some of the oldest homes in Fresno County while the Mennonite Quilting Center and downtown shops offer turn-of-the-century charm. The EdgeWater is the closest inn to Kings Canyon and Sequoia parks.

Homewood Suites Hotel

Homewood Suites Hotel
10 West Trimble Road
San Jose, CA 95131
800-CALL-HOME
(408) 428-9900

Room Rates:	$69–$179, including a continental breakfast, AAA and AARP discounts.
Pet Charges or Deposits:	$75 per day and $200 deposit; pets up to 30 lbs.
Rated: 3 Paws 🐾🐾🐾	140 suites, business center, conference facilities, secretarial services, heated pool, whirlpool, sports court, exercise room, laundry facilities, in-room data ports, airport transportation, convenience store, manager's reception.

T he spacious, apartment-style accommodations of Homewood Suites offer guests separate living and sleeping areas, furnished with the amenities of home such as remote-controlled televisions, a VCR, data ports, voice-mail message system and a fully equipped kitchen. The expanded continental breakfast and evening social hour in the Lodge are opportunities to mingle with other guests.

After breakfast, guests may choose to lounge by the pool or swim a few laps, work out in the exercise center, join in a game at the sports/activity court or head out for a day of thrills at the nearby Great America Theme Park.

Business travelers will appreciate the 24-hour executive center with use of personal computers, modem and copier, secretarial services, free incoming faxes, discounted outgoing faxes and Federal Express drop-off sites.

The Westin Hotel

Santa Clara Westin Hotel
5101 Great America Parkway
Santa Clara, CA 95054
800-WESTIN-1
(408) 986-0700

Room Rates: $109–$199, AAA discounts.
Pet Charges or Deposits: None
Rated: 4 Paws 🐾🐾🐾🐾 520 rooms and suites, business center, conference facilities, heated pool, sauna, whirlpool, 18-hole golf, tennis courts, exercise facilities, restaurant and cocktail lounge, 24-hour room service, in-room coffee makers, honor bars and refrigerators.

L ocated in the heart of Silicon Valley, next to Paramount's Great America Theme Park and near the Santa Clara Valley vineyards, the Santa Clara Westin Hotel is a popular destination for both business and leisure travelers. The 14-story facility offers 500 rooms and 20 suites equipped with creature comforts of home and a luxury hotel. Eight Westin Guest Offices outfit business travelers with high-tech office setups and services.

Enjoy the flavor and activities of the area by visiting Northern California's preeminent theme park, featuring rides and entertainment. If golf or tennis is more your style, the Santa Clara Golf and Tennis Club is next door and features a par 72 championship golf course and tennis center, both with professional instructors. To keep fit away from home guests can work out in the hotel's private fitness center with exercise equipment, sauna, heated outdoor pool with whirlpool spa. There are even jogging and hiking trails nearby. For your dog's enjoyment, there is an exercise area at the hotel and a park nearby.

Ocean Front Vacation Rental

Ocean Front Vacation Rental
1600 West Cliff Drive
Santa Cruz, CA 95060
800-801-4453
(408) 266-4453

Room Rates:	$1,200–$1,450 per week
Pet Charges or Deposits:	$200 refundable deposit
Rated: 4 Paws 🐾🐾🐾🐾	3 bedroom/2 bath home, sleeps up to eight people, full kitchen.

If you're looking for a real "home away from home" for a relaxing family vacation at the beach or an extended business trip, this furnished Ocean Front Vacation Rental may be ideal. Many vacationers choose these accommodations because they enjoy cooking for themselves and prefer the homelike surroundings, with enclosed back yard and ocean views. Pets are welcome, but should not to be left alone in the house or yard. A list of pet sitters is available.

Guests may venture along miles of shoreline flanked by prestigious West Cliff Drive and explore secluded beaches with their pets. Or if you like amusement parks, head over to the Santa Cruz Beach and Boardwalk for a day of entertainment before returning to relax in front of a roaring fire as you watch the sun go down.

Visit their website at http://www.OceanFrontHouse.com for additional information and pictures.

Ocean Pacific Lodge

Ocean Pacific Lodge
120 Washington Street
Santa Cruz, CA 95060
800-995-0289
(408) 457-1234

Room Rates: $60–$125, including continental breakfast, AAA and AARP discounts.

Pet Charges or Deposits: $10 fee; small pets only.

Rated: 3 Paws 🐾🐾🐾 68 rooms and suites, heated pool, meeting and banquet facilities, laundry facilities, exercise room, close to the ocean and boardwalk.

L ocated just two blocks from the beach, Ocean Pacific Lodge offers comfortable accommodations in the heart of Santa Cruz's beach resort community. For guests mixing business with pleasure, the lodge offers in-room fax and computer hookups and fully equipped meeting facilities. The lodge features large rooms and suites, many with in-room micro-fridges, as well as a complimentary continental breakfast.

Walk to the Beach and Boardwalk for a day of sun, fun, midway games and amusement park rides or visit the downtown area's restaurants and unique shops. The area boasts numerous parks and beaches for a picnic, a day of beachcombing or a game of catch with your dog.

Paraiso Hot Springs

Paraiso Hot Springs
Soledad, CA 93960
(408) 678-2882

Room Rates:	$110–$200
Pet Charges or Deposits:	$5–$15 per day and $50 per unit deposit.
Rated: 4 Paws 🐾🐾🐾🐾	Cabins and cottages range from studios to large houses, all with private baths and kitchens, Olympic-sized swimming pool, 3 mineral pools, exercise room, recreation room, lodge and lounge, snack bar, picnic and barbecue area, hiking trails, camping and trailer area, wineries, grocery stores and restaurants nearby.

Nestled among 280 acres overlooking the renowned Salinas Valley is the rustic, secluded resort known as Paraiso Hot Springs. On what was originally a 1790 Spanish land grant, Franciscan padres established a mission, La Nuestra de La Soledad, at the hot springs to take advantage of the healing nature of the mineral baths. Nearly 200 years later, a hotel was established, but later burned to the ground. Today the resort is being slowly restored while guests, too, become revitalized in the springs and serenity.

Here guests will discover a relaxing atmosphere for the whole family, including pets. You may spend the day by the Olympic-style pool, soak in the enclosed hot baths or mineral pools, visit the old bathhouse that houses two tiled tubs filled with therapeutic waters ranging from 102-108 degrees or pack a picnic lunch and explore the area.

The Redwoods Guest Cottages

The Redwoods Guest Cottages
8038 Chilnualna Falls Road
Yosemite National Park, CA 95389
(209) 375-6666

Room Rates:	$82–$345
Pet Charges or Deposits:	None
Rated: 3 Paws ❧❧❧	125 fully equipped rustic cottages and modern homes, spacious decks and fireplaces, located in Yosemite National Park.

The Redwoods Guest Cottages offers lodging choices ranging from rustic one-bedroom cottages and cabins to spacious, modern five-bedroom homes, all nestled among the forest and mountain streams of Wawona.

In winter, visitors revel in spectacular skiing at Badger Pass. Spring brings rebirth to the park's natural bounty, especially the waterfalls at Chilnualna Falls. Summer is the perfect time to rent a horse or take a stagecoach ride at Wawona Stables, play a round of golf at Wawona Golf Course or wet your fishing line in one of the many streams and creeks. In the fall, enjoy the crisp days and colorful changes in the foliage and nights around a campfire. No matter what the season, nature is at your doorstep in Yosemite.

WHERE TO TAKE YOUR PET IN
Central California

Leashes are required unless otherwise stated.

APTOS

Rio Del Mar Beach is a wide, sandy strip of beach on Rio Del Mar Boulevard. There is plenty of room for you and Rover to stretch your legs and get your feet wet. For more information, call (408) 688-3222.

CARMEL AND CARMEL VALLEY

(See North Pacific Coast Highway – The Monterey Peninsula)

ELKHORN SLOUGH NATIONAL WETLANDS RESERVE AND SANCTUARY

Situated near Moss Landing (between Castroville and Watsonville) off Highway 1, you can take as long as several hours to explore this vast home to native flora and fauna. There are hundreds of species of birds, small mammals and fish. A visitors' center demonstrates both the history of the sanctuary and the uses of wetlands throughout the United States. You and your pet walk on boardwalks which are slightly above the wetlands themselves. Take plenty of film for this adventure. Nearby Moss Landing, commercial fishing hub of Monterey Bay, has numerous antique shops, excellent seafood restaurants, and the ambiance of an Italian fishing village. For more information, call (408) 728-5939.

FRESNO

Kearney Park was formerly a 225-acre estate and is now a scenic park. The exquisite mansion and the ancient trees are a sight to behold. The park is 7 miles west of Fresno on Kearney Boulevard. There is a small fee.

Kings River Special Management Area is a wild trout fishery in the Kings River. This exceptional recreational area consists of 49,000 acres in the Sierra and Sequoia National Forests. Take Belmont Avenue east, which turns into Trimmer Springs Road, and continue around Pine Flat Reservoir, past Kirch Flat Campground, over the bridge and along the Kings River to the Special Management Area. For more information, call (209) 855-8321.

Pine Flat Lake is a wonderful area for a day of picnicking and playing with your dog. Here you will find incredible views, a trickling stream, ancient oak trees and a beautiful blue lake. If you are a fisherman, you might want to wet your line. To reach the lake, take Belmont Avenue east, which turns into Trimmer Springs Road, and follow it for 35 miles to the lake. For more information, call (209) 787-2589.

Woodward Park consists of 300 acres of lush fields, woods, lakes and streams to explore. The park is also a bird refuge, so you may want to bring your binoculars, too. Take Highway 41 and exit at Friant Road, head northeast, then turn left on East Audubon Drive and continue to the main entrance. There is a parking fee. For more information, call (209) 498-1551.

HALF MOON BAY

Bean Hallow State Beach is off of Highway 1 south, 18 miles from town. There is a level projection above the beach where you can explore and watch the sea lions. For more information, call (415) 879-0832.

Davenport Beach is full of untouched sand dunes and breathtaking ocean views. This is a chance for your dog to run leash-free. Head south on Highway 1, past Ano Nuevo State Park for 9 miles to Davenport. There you will find plenty of parking along the highway. For more information, call (408) 462-8333.

McNee Ranch State Park has spectacular views from several trails ranging from sea level to nearly 2,000 feet. It can get warm, so bring enough water for both you and your pooch. For more information, call (916) 653-6995.

MERCED

There are several neighborhood parks with plenty of running room:
Ada Givens Park, at Hawthorn Avenue and Ada Givens School
Applegate Park, between "M" and "R" Streets
Burbank Park, at Olive Avenue and Burbank School
Circle Drive Park, at East 23rd Street and Circle Drive
Courthouse Park, at 21st and "M" streets
Fahrens Park, at Buena Vista Drive
Flanagan Park, at East Cone Avenue
Gilbert Macias Park, at Child Avenue and "G" Street
Joe Herb Park, at Yosemite Parkway and Parsons
McNamara Park, at 11th and Canal streets
McReady Park, at Grogan Avenue and McReady Drive
Rahilly Park, at Parsons Avenue and Flying Circle
Santa Fe Strip Park, at Buena Vista Drive and "M" Street
Stephen Leonard Park, at 7th and "T" streets

North Pacific Coast Highway – The Monterey Peninsula

MONTEREY

Jack's Peak Regional Park, off of Highway 68 on Jack's Peak Road, offers 8.5 miles of paths and trails to wander, plus panoramic views of Carmel Valley and Monterey Bay from Monterey Peninsula's highest point. For more information, call (408) 755-4899.

Monterey and Pacific Grove share a wonderful, scenic walking/jogging and bike path that stretches from Lover's Point on Sunset Drive in Pacific Grove, around the cliffs that hug the Monterey Bay, through Monterey's famed Cannery Row, and on past Fisherman's Wharf along Del Monte Avenue, ending at Canyon Del Rey.

PACIFIC GROVE

Asilomar State Beach, on Sunset Drive between Monterey and Pebble Beach, offers a stretch of rugged coastline to explore and remarkable tide pools. For more information, call (408) 372-4076.

George Washington Park is leash-free from sunrise to 9 a.m. and 4 p.m. to sunset. It is full of tall pine trees, picnic tables and is a popular hangout for locals and their dogs. It is bordered by Melrose Avenue, Short Street, Alder Street and Pine Avenue. For more information, call (408) 648-3100.

Lynn "Rip" Van Winkle Open Space is leash-free from sunrise to 9 a.m. and 4 p.m. to sunset. There is plenty of open space and lots of trails to explore. Located across from Forest Grove Elementary School, just outside of the non-toll section of Seventeen Mile Drive, the entrance is a small, dirt parking lot on your right. Take Sunset Drive, turn right on Congress Avenue. The unmarked parking area is on the right, just past the school.

CARMEL

Carmel City Beach is off of Highway 1 at the bottom of Ocean Avenue. Here you and your pet can enjoy a leash-free romp, a dip in the water or a stroll along the cypress-lined walking path together. For more information, call (408) 624-3543.

CARMEL VALLEY

Garland Ranch Regional Park, off of Highway 1 on Carmel Valley Road, is great if wide-open spaces are more to your liking. This leash-free paradise is comprised of 9 miles of scenic trails and 4,500 acres of oak, willow and maple trees. It's an outdoor experience you and your pup will never forget. For more information, call (408) 659-4488.

BIG SUR

Pfeiffer Big Sur State Beach is off of Highway 1 on narrow, winding Sycamore Canyon Road. Enjoy the awe-inspiring view from the white sand beaches as the treacherous waves of the Pacific Ocean crash against the rocks, sea caves and natural arches. Leashes are required. For more information, call (408) 648-3130.

REEDLEY

Hillcrest Tree Farm is a peaceful little park for you and your dog to explore. It is on Reed Road at Adams, north of Reedley.

Pioneer Park is a nice place to pack a lunch and spend the day with your four-legged friend. This neighborhood park is on the corner of "G" and 8th streets.

SAN JOSE

Almaden Quicksilver County Park has 3,600 acres and 15 miles of trails to explore. There is a wonderful picnic area and lots of wildflowers. Take Highway 85 to the Almaden Expressway exit south for 4.5 miles to Almaden Road to Mockingbird Hill Lane and turn right and follow it to the parking area. For more information, call (408) 268-3883.

Anderson Lake Park is 2,365 acres of open space. Here you will find a great 15-mile pathway that wanders along the Coyote Creek through the trees and abundant wildlife. If you like fly fishing, you will enjoy trying your luck at Coyote Creek, which is open for fishing April to November. The Anderson Reservoir is a great place to wet your line, too. The park can be accessed from Cochrane Road in Morgan Hill, east of Highway 101 to Monterey Road until you reach Burnett Avenue. There is an entry fee posted at the gate. For more information, call (408) 779-3634.

Calero Park has wonderful views of the Santa Cruz Mountains. It is a great place for a picnic and is full of wildflowers in the spring. It is good place for fishing if you like to catch and release; it is not advisable to eat the fish. Dogs are not allowed on the beach, but there is plenty of room to explore. Take Almaden Expressway south to Harry Road, turn right, then left on McKean Road to reach the park entrance. For more information, call (408)268-3883.

Coyote Hellyer Park is 223 beautiful acres west of the Hellyer Avenue exit along Highway 101. Wander along the stream, through the tall trees and get back to nature. It is a great place for a picnic or a barbecue with the family. There is a 15-mile hike along Coyote Creek that leads to Anderson Park. The entrance fee is posted at the ranger station. For more information, call (408) 225-0225.

Joseph D. Grant County Park is in the Diablo Range of the Coastal Mountains. The views are spectacular and so is the wildlife. It is a wonderful place to hike in the spring when the wildflowers are in bloom. Fees are posted at the park entrance. The areas that allow dogs are posted, too. To reach the park, take Mount Hamilton Road to the east for 8 miles to Alum Rock Avenue. For more information, call (408) 274-6121.

Kelley Park is popular with the locals. There are great walking paths for you and your dog to explore. There is a parking fee on holidays and weekends. The park is on Senter Road, between Tully Road and Keyes Street.

Lexington County Park encompasses a 450-acre lake where you can spend the day boating or fishing or just enjoying the surrounding scenery with your dog. The fees are posted at the entrance. Dogs are restricted to certain areas. To reach the park, take Interstate 880 to Old Santa Cruz Highway and continue on to Aldercroft Heights Road. This leads to Alma Bridge Road; follow that to the parking area. For more information, call (408) 867-0190.

At Penitencia Creek County Park, several small parks were combined to make an 83-acre park along the Penitencia Creek. It is great for a relaxing picnic with your dog. Fees are posted at the entrance. The park is bounded by Noble Avenue, Jackson and Mabury streets. Dogs are restricted to certain areas. For more information, call (408) 358-3741.

SANTA CLARA

Central Park, off of Kiely Boulevard, has 52 acres of trails to wander. It is a great place to soak up some sun or have a picnic.

Lexington Reservoir, off of Highway 17 at Alma Bridge Road, is a lovely park where you and your dog can fish, swim or spend the day exploring the park. For more information, call (408) 358-3741.

Santa Clara Dog Park, the only leash-free park in Santa Clara, is at 3445 Lochinvar Avenue near Lawrence Expressway and Homestead Road. This is a dog's paradise. Here he can run and play with other dogs. There are pooper scoopers, fresh water and a small enclosed dog run with benches for the humans.

SANTA CRUZ

Bonny Doon Beach, off of Highway 1 on Bonny Doon Road, is an isolated, peaceful beach surrounded with high bluffs. It is a great place to spend the day beachcombing, playing fetch with your dog or picnicking. For more information, call (408) 462-8333.

East Cliff Drive offers several access areas to dog-friendly beaches. Starting around 12th Street to 41st, there are periodical streets leading to several beaches. Try the beach off of Seabright between the Boardwalk and the Yacht Harbor.

Mitchell's Cove Beach, on West Cliff Drive between Almar and Woodrow avenues, offers you and your dog an opportunity to romp the beach leash-free from dawn to 10 a.m. and 4 p.m. to sunset.

Pleasure Point Beach is off of East Cliff Drive on Pleasure Point Drive. This is a surfers' paradise, but your pooch will love it, too. Climb down the staircase to access the sandy beach or walk the trail around the cliff for a bird's-eye view.

West Lighthouse Beach, on West Cliff Drive, is leash-free from dawn to 10 a.m. and 4 p.m. to sunset. It is a nice stretch of beach for a run or just a good game of Frisbee. For more information, call (408) 429-3777.

SEQUOIA AND KINGS CANYON NATIONAL PARK

The park's 1,139,519 acres are scattered with the largest living sequoia trees, many reaching more than 30 feet in diameter and more than 200 feet tall, as well as with magnificent forests of ponderosa and sugar pine trees. The park extends from the foothill of the San Joaquin Valley to the crest of the High Sierras with the highest point reaching 14,494 feet. The wildlife ranges from mule deer to the common chipmunk, so your dog will have a ball with all of the creature smells. Here you and your dog can go camping, picnicking, hiking, boating, fishing, swimming or horseback riding. There also are nature programs and a visitors center. Dogs are not allowed on trails or in public buildings. There are several ways to access the park and many more things to see and do. It is recommended that you call the superintendent of the park for directions, recreation and camping information at (209) 565-3134.

YOSEMITE NATIONAL PARK

Set aside as the nation's first state park by Abraham Lincoln on June 30, 1864, Yosemite became a national park 26 years later. This region of unusual, breathtaking, natural beauty lies in Central California on the western slope of the Sierra Nevada and consists of 1,169 square miles of land. There are more than 800 miles of trails to explore and more streams, creeks and rivers than you could fish in a week. The main paved route to Yosemite is SR 140 from Merced. At the park, you can go camping, hiking, fishing, boating, bicycling, swimming, river rafting and horseback riding. There are plenty of food service areas, visitors centers, lodges and different types of cabins. Dogs and cats are welcome in the park in the Upper Pines, in Yosemite Valley, the west end of the campgrounds at Tuolumne Meadows, at White Wolf, Bridalveil Falls, Crane Flat, Wawona, Hodgdon Meadows, and Yosemite Creek campgrounds. They are not allowed on trails or in public buildings. For information on the park, its restrictions on pets and accommodations, call the park superintendent at (209) 372-0200 or 372-0265.

Southern California

Residence Inn by Marriott

Residence Inn by Marriott
1700 S. Clementine Street
Anaheim, CA 92802
800-331-3131
(714) 533-3555

Room Rates:	$169–$229, including breakfast buffet, AAA and AARP discounts.
Pet Charges or Deposits:	$6 per day and $275 deposit.
Rated: 3 Paws 🐾🐾🐾	200 rooms and suites with fully equipped kitchens and some fireplaces, daily maid service, grocery shopping service, heated pool, whirlpool, Sport Court, health club privileges, meeting facilities, complimentary evening beverage.

Located near major Southern California attractions, the Anaheim Residence Inn by Marriott will appeal to business travelers and vacationers alike. From spacious accommodations with separate sleeping and living areas, the fully equipped kitchens, grocery shopping service, laundry facilities, room service from any of the local restaurants, work areas and meeting facilities to the manager-hosted continental breakfast buffet and informal hospitality hour, the inn seems more like a home than a hotel.

For recreation, the retreat offers a heated swimming pool, whirlpool, toddlers' pool, barbecue areas and a Sport Court where you can play a game of basketball, volleyball or tennis. Your pet can join you for a stroll around the groomed grounds.

Residence Inn by Marriott

Residence Inn by Marriott
321 E. Huntington Drive
Arcadia, CA 91006
800-331-3131
(818) 446-6500

Room Rates: $112–$142, including breakfast buffet, AAA and AARP discounts.
Pet Charges or Deposits: $6 per night; additional pets $3; plus $50-$75 deposit.
Rated: 3 Paws 🐾🐾🐾 120 rooms and studios, some with fireplaces, fully equipped kitchens, meeting rooms, heated pool, whirlpool and Sport Court.

I f you're looking for that "at home" feeling, look no further than the Residence Inn by Marriott. Whether you choose an oversized studio or a two-bed penthouse suite, all accommodations offer a fully equipped kitchen, microwave and comfortable living area. Guests will enjoy the complimentary grocery shopping service, satellite television, laundry facilities, valet service, curbside parking, shuttle service and more.

After a hard day at work or play, unwind with a game of basketball or tennis on the Sport Court, take a swim in the heated pool, relax in the whirlpool or take the dog for a stroll on the pet walk. The evening hospitality hour, weekly manager's barbecue and neighborhood setting add a social flavor to your stay.

Residence Inn by Marriott

Residence Inn by Marriott
4241 Chester Lane
Bakersfield, CA 93309
800-331-3131
(805) 321-9800

Room Rates:	$65–$119, including breakfast, AAA discounts.
Pet Charges or Deposits:	$6 per day and $60 deposit/cleaning fee
Rated: 4 Paws 🐾🐾🐾🐾	114 suites, 52 with fireplaces, central courtyard, meeting rooms, putting green, exercise room and Sport Court.

C onsistently rated among the top 20 hotels in the nation, Residence Inn by Marriott is a leader in extended stay lodging for families and business travelers. Here you'll discover a warm, homey feeling the minute you walk into the townhouse-like building.

With amenities such as a complimentary breakfast buffet, evening hospitality hour, weekly barbecue or dinner, spacious suites with full kitchens, guest laundry facilities and computer hookups, you will feel right at home. The landscaped grounds, walkways and a central courtyard foster a community setting. For recreation, there are a pool with heated spa, a Sport Court for tennis, basketball and volleyball and a putting green so you can get in some practice before you hit the course. There are also dog runs and exercise areas for your pet's recreational and exercise needs, too.

Regent Beverly Wilshire

Regent Beverly Wilshire
9500 Wilshire Boulevard
Beverly Hills, CA 90212
800-545-4000
(310) 275-5200

Room Rates:	$265 and up
Pet Charges or Deposits:	None
Rated: 4 Paws 🐾 🐾 🐾 🐾	279 elegant rooms, business center, meeting and conference facilities, heated pool, saunas, whirlpool, health club, valet laundry service, 24-hour room service, coffee shop, restaurant and cocktail lounge.

L ocated in the heart of Beverly Hills, the historic Regent Beverly Wilshire hotel's 275 generously proportioned guest rooms have housed dignitaries, celebrities and discerning travelers since 1928. The attention to detail is evident by the services of the 24-hour personal room attendants, the attentive concierge staff, the oversized and understated rooms, the use of natural fabrics and hues, the opulent bathrooms with their deep soaking tubs and separate showers, the plush terry robes, premium toiletries, dual phone lines and executive-sized desks.

Nothing is overlooked, including your pet. Upon arrival, canine guests receive a dish of biscuits and bottled water to make their stay more comfortable.

For your dining pleasure, select from the creative California-continental cuisine in the Dining Room, have cappuccino overlooking Rodeo Drive in the Café, high tea or cocktails in the European ambiance of the Lobby Lounge or a brandy in The Bar.

Walker River Lodge

Walker River Lodge
100 Main Street
Bridgeport, CA 93517
800-688-3351
(760) 932-7021

Room Rates:	$45–$120
Pet Charges or Deposits:	None
Rated: 3 Paws 🐾🐾🐾	36 rooms and suites, landscaped grounds, whirlpool, heated pool, refrigerators, some microwaves, gift shop.

Walker River Lodge is nestled in the valley of the Eastern Sierras in the historic town of Bridgeport. Located directly on the East Walker River, many rooms face the riverfront where guests may take advantage of some of the finest trout fishing in the Sierras.

Guests will appreciate the large, comfortable accommodations, satellite television, heated pool and spa. For non-fishing guests, there are plenty of sights to see: the Bodie Ghost Town, Mono Lake, Twin Lakes, Virginia Lakes, snow skiing in the winter, the natural hot springs and Yosemite National Park. Or opt to relax by the peaceful river with a picnic lunch or barbecue.

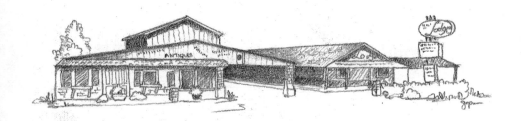

Airport Hilton and Convention Center

Airport Hilton and Convention Center
2500 Hollywood Way
Burbank, CA 91505
800-445-8667
(818) 843-6000

Room Rates:	$120–$480, AAA and AARP discounts.
Pet Charges or Deposits:	$50 deposit.
Rated: 3 Paws 🐾🐾🐾	500 luxury rooms and suites, some with fireplaces and mountain views, 2 pools, exercise room, meeting facilities, airport transportation, cocktail lounge, dining room and coffee shop.

The Burbank Airport Hilton and Convention Center, near Southern California attractions, offers guests hospitality, spacious suites with panoramic mountains views, meeting facilities and convenience.

The hotel is 10 minutes from Universal Studios, 30 minutes to Magic Mountain and 50 minutes to Disneyland. Before or after taking in local attractions, enjoy the hotel's saunas, spas or pools. Or if you are up for a workout, head to the hotel's fitness center.

For dining and entertainment, visit famous Lew's Restaurant and Lounge. Here you can enjoy casual dining while listening to live music from the piano bar.

La Quinta Inn

La Quinta Inn
150 Bonita Road
Chula Vista, CA 91910
800-531-5900
(619) 691-1211

Room Rates:	$71–$89, including light breakfast, AAA and AARP discounts.
Pet Charges or Deposits:	None, small pets only.
Rated: 3 Paws 🐾🐾🐾	141 rooms, expanded in-room entertainment system, refrigerators and microwaves, meeting and conference facilities, swimming pools, game room.

F or business travelers or vacationers, the La Quinta Inn offers spacious rooms with plenty of amenities. From the crisp white exterior, softly colored lobby and relaxing atmosphere, guests will feel right at home in quiet, comfortable accommodations.

Kids of all ages will enjoy the latest video games and in-room first-run movies viewed on the expanded entertainment system. You and your dog will appreciate the landscaped, spacious grounds.

Included in the price of your accommodations is a complimentary breakfast, featuring your choice of cereal, fresh fruit, bagels, pastries, juice, milk and coffee. You can work off your breakfast at the health club.

Residence Inn by Marriott

Residence Inn by Marriott
881 W. Baker Street
Costa Mesa, CA 92626
800-331-3131
(714) 241-8800

Room Rates:	$94–$129, including breakfast buffet, AAA, AARP, AKC and ABA discounts.
Pet Charges or Deposits:	$6 per day and $40–$60 deposit.
Rated: 3 Paws ❀❀❀	144 rooms and suites with fully equipped kitchens, oversized living areas, many with fireplaces, large work desks, grocery shopping service, fitness center, Sport Court, barbecue grills, pet exercise area.

Near Disneyland and beaches, the Residence Inn affords a home-away-from-home type of environment. The spacious rooms and suites, many with wood-burning fireplaces, equipped kitchens, oversized living area, separate sleeping areas and daily housekeeping service make this inn a convenient place to stay whether traveling for business or pleasure.

A great way to get to know your neighbors and enjoy a meal is to take advantage of the breakfast buffet and complimentary hospitality hour during the week with a light buffet dinner and drinks, which are both included as part of your room rate. Barbecue grills located throughout the property are an opportunity for a dining change of pace.

The expansive, beautifully landscaped grounds and selected exercise areas are a welcome relief from the ordinary hotels for both you and your pet.

The Westin South Coast Plaza

The Westin South Coast Plaza
686 Anton Boulevard
Costa Mesa, CA 92626
800-WESTIN-1
(714) 540-2500

Room Rates:	$145–$225, AAA and AARP discounts.
Pet Charges or Deposits:	None; small pets only, manager's approval required.
Rated: 4 Paws 🐾🐾🐾🐾	373 deluxe rooms and 17 luxury suites, all with honor bars, coffee makers, large work desk, data ports, irons and ironing boards, hair dryer, children's recreational program, outdoor heated pool, sun deck, lighted tennis courts, fitness center, valet and laundry service, 24-hour room service, meeting and conference facilities, grand ballroom, covered and valet parking, gift shop, restaurant and lounge.

Situated in the heart of the Southern California's cultural, entertainment and metropolitan area, the Westin South Coast Plaza offers guests oversized guest rooms, world-class luxury suites with amenities and personalized service.

For leisure, there's a children's recreational program, pool and sun deck, jogging trails, tennis courts and a fully equipped fitness center. Or take advantage of the guest access to the Spa at South Coast Plaza, only a short stroll from the hotel across the Unity Bridge.

With more than 50 restaurants within walking distance to the hotel, there are dining options for every palate. The hotel's Garden Court Restaurant offers menus for breakfast, lunch, dinner and with an à la carte Sunday brunch. The Lobby Lounge is the place to unwind with a cocktail and appetizers before dinner.

Welk Resort Center

Welk Resort Center
8860 Lawrence Welk Drive
Escondido, CA 92026
800-932-9355
(760) 749-3000

Room Rates:	$110, AAA, AARP, AKC and ABA discounts.
Pet Charges or Deposits:	$100 deposit, $75 returnable.
Rated: 3 Paws 🐾🐾🐾	132 rooms, some with refrigerators, meeting facilities, putting green, 18-hole executive golf courses, pro shop, 2 pools, whirlpools, valet laundry, Lawrence Welk Resort Theater and Museum, coffee shop, deli, buffet dinner theater, restaurant and lounge.

T he Welk Resort Center is set on 1,000 scenic acres of rugged, unspoiled hills and valleys. Each of the spacious rooms has a panoramic view of the golf course and surrounding hills, a private patio or balcony, a micro-fridge and many other amenities.

The resort offers guests their choice of endless activity or complete serenity. Play golf on one of the three meticulously maintained 18-hole courses, relax in the sun by the pool or in one of the spas, enjoy a tennis match or take your dog for a hike in the surrounding hills.

At the Lawrence Welk Resort Theater and Museum you can enjoy lunch or dinner as well as entertaining Broadway musicals with professional casts. For dining anytime of the day, the Resort Restaurant offers an extensive selection of home-cooked entrees.

Joshua Tree Bed and Breakfast Inn

Joshua Tree Inn
61259 Twenty-nine Palms Highway
Joshua Tree, CA 92252
800-366-1444
(619) 366-1188

Room Rates: $85–$220, AAA, AARP, AKC and ABA discounts.
Pet Charges or Deposits: $10 per day. Horse corrals are available.
Rated: 3 Paws 🐾🐾🐾   10 comfortable rooms and semi-suites, with private showers,
                       full suites with complete kitchens and baths, all furnished with
                       antiques and old west memorabilia, a main living room, dining
                       room, study, patio and pool.

Minutes from the gateway to the scenic 500,000-acre Joshua Tree National Park is the Joshua Tree Bed and Breakfast Inn. This high-desert retreat strives to make you feel right at home with its charming antique furnishings and gourmet home-cooked breakfast prepared from scratch.

If you and your dog are feeling adventurous, box lunches are available for the asking, so you can spend the day exploring Joshua Tree National Park with its mines, man-made dam, endless trails for hiking or horseback riding and even geological tours.

For a romantic evening, a candlelight dinner under the stars can be arranged. The desert nights are famous for their clear sky and panoramic views. For an evening of entertainment, the Hi-Desert Playhouse is right next door and is known for first-rate theatrical productions.

Prophet's Paradise Bed and Breakfast

Prophet's Paradise Bed and Breakfast
26845 Modoc Lane
Lake Arrowhead, CA 92352
800-987-2231
(909) 336-1969

Room Rates:	$90–$160, including gourmet breakfast.
Pet Charges or Deposits:	$10 per day; no large pets; manager's approval required.
Rated: 3 Paws 🐾🐾🐾	4 spacious rooms with private baths, some with fireplaces, decorated with antiques, game room, gym, exercise area for pets.

Set in the beautiful mountain resort of Lake Arrowhead is Prophet's Paradise Bed and Breakfast. This multi-leveled inn offers four uniquely decorated rooms with antiques, oak and wicker furnishings, stained glass, featherbeds and intimate decks from which to enjoy your gourmet breakfast. All rooms have private baths, some have wood-burning fireplaces, refrigerator and wet bar.

Having been in the motion picture business for years, the innkeepers kindly share their collection of memorabilia and artifacts with their guests. You are welcome to enjoy the billiard room, work out in the gym, play horseshoes or swing under the giant oak tree. There are wonderful winding paths for you and your dog to explore with hewn logs for benches to stop for rest or repose.

Quails Inn at Lake San Marcos Resort

Quails Inn at Lake San Marcos Resort
1025 La Bonita Drive
Lake San Marcos, CA 92069
800-447-6556
(760) 744-0120

Room Rates:	$83–$250, AAA and AARP Discounts.
Pet Charges or Deposits:	$10 per day; small pets only; manager's approval required.
Rated: 3 Paws 🐾🐾🐾	142 lakeside room and apartments with balcony or patio, 16 with wet bar, refrigerator, whirlpool baths, meeting rooms, 2 heated pools, whirlpool, boating, tennis courts, exercise room, golf courses.

S an Diego's only lakeside resort, The Quails Inn offers distinctive lakeside rooms and comfortable suites.

There are a variety of activities to keep you entertained, including tennis, swimming, boating and canoeing on the mile-long lake. If golf is your game, try the resort's 72-par championship course or the hilly par-58 executive course.

Spacious one- or-two bedroom lakeside apartments, complete with kitchenette, dining and sitting areas are near Southern California attractions and the heart of San Diego. For on-site dining, guests may choose either of the acclaimed Quails Inn Dinnerhouse or the Country Club Restaurant.

Residence Inn by Marriott

Residence Inn by Marriott
8901 Gilman Drive
La Jolla, CA 92037
800-531-5900
(619) 587-1770

Room Rates:	$95–$189, including breakfast buffet, AAA and AARP discounts.
Pet Charges or Deposits:	$6 per day and $25-$50 cleaning fee.
Rated: 3 Paws ❀❀❀	287 rooms and suites, all with living rooms and separate sleeping areas, some with fireplaces, meeting facilities, 2 heated pools, whirlpool, Sport Court, complimentary evening beverages, laundry facilities, airport transportation, pet exercise area.

When it comes to a relaxation and affordable accommodations with all the amenities of home, look no further than Residence Inn by Marriott. And since pet owners would not feel at home unless the "entire family" was along, the inn has allocated certain Pet Suites. Here await comfortable rooms and suites more inviting than an ordinary hotel. That's likely due to the wood-burning fireplace, separate sleeping and living areas, the grocery shopping service and the complimentary hospitality hours during the week.

Start the day with the breakfast buffet served at the Gatehouse, followed by a day of sightseeing, a visit to some of the major attractions or stay where you are and relax by the pool, swim a few laps or venture to the Sport Court for a game of tennis, volleyball or basketball. Pets have their own exercise area, too.

San Diego Marriott

San Diego Marriott
4240 La Jolla Village Drive
La Jolla, CA 92037
800-228-9290
(619) 587-1414

Room Rates:	$198–$650, AARP discounts.
Pet Charges or Deposits:	Credit card imprint only.
Rated: 4 Paws 🐾🐾🐾🐾	360 rooms and 11 luxury suites, whirlpool, saunas, indoor and outdoor pools, health club, game room, restaurants, cocktail lounge, valet parking, ballroom, meeting and conference facilities, gift shop, close to major attractions.

S ituated in the heart of La Jolla's business district and minutes from major attractions, the La Jolla – San Diego Marriott offers impeccable service and striking elegance combined with business and banquet facilities. The climate-controlled rooms and luxury suites offer guests amenities that range from the basics to Concierge Level upgrades.

Dining options include JW's Sea Grill with indoor and outdoor seating or Character's Bar and Grill for sports action. The San Diego Marriott – La Jolla prides itself on being a hotel big enough for an impressive reception or business conference, yet small enough for personal service.

Residence Inn by Marriott

Residence Inn by Marriott
14419 Firestone Boulevard
La Mirada, CA 90638
800-331-3131
(714) 523-2800

Room Rates:	$135–$160, including breakfast buffet, AAA, AARP, AKC and ABA discounts.
Pet Charges or Deposits:	$5 per pet per day; $100-$200 deposit; Limit two pets up to 35 pounds.
Rated: 3 Paws 🐾🐾🐾	146 suites with fully equipped kitchens, pool, Jacuzzi, exercise room, Sport Court, laundry facilities, meeting facilities, business services, room service, manager-hosted evening hospitality, near all major attractions.

If you need accommodations for a short business trip or an extended family vacation that offer plenty of space and the comforts of home, then La Mirada's Residence Inn fits the bill. Here your suite will be larger than the normal hotel room, with the convenience of a fully equipped kitchen and private sleeping area.

Start your morning with a refreshing Gatehouse breakfast. For aquatic relaxation, the pool or the Jacuzzi may call you. For a workout, the inn's exercise room has all the equipment you will need or join some of the other guests in a game of basketball or tennis on the Sport Court. You and your pet can enjoy a stroll through the manicured grounds before you head out for a day of business, sightseeing or visiting some of the area's major attractions. Top off your day with complimentary evening beverages and hors d'oeuvres served either in the Gatehouse or poolside.

La Quinta Inn

La Quinta Inn
3 Centerpointe Drive
La Palma, CA 90623
800-687-6667
(714) 670-1400

Room Rates: $47–$58, including light breakfast, AAA discounts.
Pet Charges or Deposits: None.
Rated: 3 Paws ❖ ❖ ❖   159 rooms and suites, many with balconies, fitness room,
conference facilities, large work areas, data ports, heated pool,
whirlpool, airport transportation, restaurant, near major
attractions.

Near most major Southern California attractions, the La Palma – La Quinta Inn offers families on vacation and business travelers all the comforts of home at a reasonable price. From the oversized bathrooms, the large work area with data port phones, to the comfortable recliners and king-size beds featured in all the rooms, the accommodations are perfect for a week or a weekend. You and your dog will appreciate the landscaped, spacious grounds.

Start the day off with the complimentary First Light breakfast, featuring your choice of cereals, fresh fruit, pastries, bagels, juice, milk and coffee.

Whether you spend your day relaxing by the pool, soaking in the whirlpool, working out in the fitness room or visiting one of the many theme parks in the area, you and your family will find plenty of adventures here.

Quality Inn and Executive Suites

Quality Inn and Executive Suites
1621 North "H" Street
Lompoc, CA 93436
800-228-5151
(805) 735-8555

Room Rates:	$59–$84, AAA discounts.
Pet Charges or Deposits:	$25 per stay
Rated: 3 Paws 🐾🐾🐾	218 rooms, some larger efficiency rooms, 91 executive suites, meeting rooms, heated pool, whirlpool, exercise area for dogs.

A t the southern end of the Central Coast Mountain Range, the Quality Inn and Executive Suites is set in the scenic Lompoc Valley. Surrounded by historic missions, fields of colorful flowers, blue skies and friendly people, guests may choose from several distinctive rooms and suites.

When choosing the "deluxe" room, guests enjoy the added bonus of a microwave and refrigerator. The "executive suite" adds a sitting area and kitchenette. Of course, all rooms and suites include in-room coffee, guest laundry facilities, full health club privileges, massage salon and use of the heated pool and spa. For guests traveling with their animals, there is a pet exercise area.

Embassy Suites Hotel

Embassy Suites Hotel
8425 Firestone Boulevard
Downey, CA 90241
800-EMBASSY
(310) 861-1900

Room Rates:	$109–$129, including full breakfast, AAA and AARP discounts.
Pet Charges or Deposits:	$15 per day and $50 nonrefundable deposit.
Rated: 3 Paws 🐾🐾🐾	219 suites with private bed and living rooms, refrigerator and microwave, indoor pool, sauna, steam room, whirlpool, exercise room, meeting rooms, secretarial services, complimentary evening beverages, restaurant, laundry service, gift shop, exercise area for dogs.

L ocated in the heart of Southern California, the Embassy Suites Hotel – Los Angeles-Downey offers guests the convenience and luxury of a first-class hotel at an affordable rate. The spacious two-room suites give you that homey feeling while offering all the added amenities a business traveler or vacationing family needs. Relax in the lush tropical gardens of the eight-story atrium courtyard with its rock waterfall and koi-filled ponds as you enjoy the manager's reception.

Awake to a complimentary morning newspaper and a full cooked-to-order breakfast. For an intimate dinner, Gregory's Restaurant overlooks the hotel's atrium and features such main dishes as Chicken Jerusalem and Steak Dijon. Top off your evening with a nightcap at Gregory's Lounge.

Four Seasons – Regent Hotel

Four Seasons – Regent Hotel
300 South Doheny Drive
Los Angeles, CA 90048
800-332-3442
(310) 273-2222

Room Rates:	$295 and up, AAA discounts.
Pet Charges or Deposits:	None; small pets only.
Rated: 4 Paws 🐾🐾🐾🐾	285 guest rooms and suites with private bar, VCR, fax machine, voice mail, multi-line phones and computer hookups, heated pool, whirlpool, exercise room, massage, twice daily maid service, 24-hour concierge services, meeting rooms, exercise area for pets, complimentary limousine service to Rodeo Drive, 24-hour room service and award winning restaurants.

O verlooking Beverly Hills and greater Los Angeles, the Four Seasons – Regent Hotel features 285 residential-style guest rooms and suites decorated with floral, Oriental, contemporary or eclectic designs. All rooms offer amenities such as refrigerated bars, computer hookup, 24-hour room and laundry services and twice daily maid service. Situated among a lush garden on the fourth floor are the outdoor swimming pool and Jacuzzi, with a tented exercise and massage center.

For award-winning dining, Gardens Restaurant offers contemporary California cuisine. For an informal menu, there's The Café or the Poolside Terrace. Top off your evening at the Windows Lounge, featuring nightly entertainment and cocktails.

Your pets will be treated to dinner service offering a choice of personal favorites prepared to their specifications before a pet care specialist takes charge of the dog-walking duties.

Hotel Bel-Air

Hotel Bel-Air
701 Stone Canyon Road
Los Angeles, CA 90071
800-648-4097
(310) 472-1211

Room Rates:	$285 and up.
Pet Charges or Deposits:	$250 fee.
Rated: 5 Paws 🐾🐾🐾🐾🐾	92 luxury rooms and suites with refrigerators, safes, cable television, landscaped grounds, heated pool, health club, meeting rooms, secretarial services, valet laundry services, restaurant and cocktail lounge with live entertainment.

The magic and charm of the Hotel Bel-Air is evident as soon as you cross over the arched bridge and enter this 1920s mission-style hotel. Situated in the prestigious Bel-Air district in a heavily wooded canyon, the two-story pink stucco structure is crowned by a bell tower and flanked by courtyards and fountains. Housed in several buildings, rooms and suites offer a variety of sizes, floor plans, views and enjoy individual entrances from the hotel gardens, fountain courtyards or the pool area. Many rooms feature hot tubs, wood-burning fireplaces, terra cotta floors and exquisite needlepoint rugs. For exercise, there's the oval-shaped pool or the 24-hour fitness center.

If you're looking for solitude, escape to the chef's working garden offering an a romantic place to relax with a book or special companion. For meals, sample alfresco dining at the bougainvillea-draped Terrace overlooking Swan Lake or try the award-winning seasonal French-California cuisine of the famed Hotel Bel-Air Restaurant. Top your evening off with a cocktail in The Bar, which features nightly piano entertainment. You will soon discover why the Hotel Bel-Air has been an oasis for celebrities and dignitaries for more than 50 years.

Hotel Nikko at Beverly Hills

Hotel Nikko at Beverly Hills
465 South La Cienega Boulevard
Los Angeles, CA 90048-4001
800-NIKKO-US
(310) 247-0400

Room Rates:	$270 and up.
Pet Charges or Deposits:	$100 deposit; manager's approval required.
Rated: 4 Paws 🐾🐾🐾🐾	304 contemporary rooms with CD stereo system, in-room fax, business and conference facilities, data ports, secretarial services, valet laundry, heated pool, saunas, exercise room, airport transportation, restaurant and cocktail lounge.

S ituated at the edge of Beverly Hills, the Hotel Nikko is only minutes from major area attractions. When entering the lobby, visitors will likely be struck by the contrast and beauty of another world. The advanced technology of this highly automated hotel is discreetly hidden by the soothing colors and simple elegance. Business travelers will appreciate the extra thought put into the design of the luxurious work environment; the perfect place for a small conference or intimate business dinner.

Upon entering your room, you will be greeted by the aroma of a fresh bouquet of flowers. The neutral palette of colors and hand-made art work make an immediate visual impression. Guests are offered the ultimate in amenities, a generous living room, a spacious bedroom, a luxurious bath and powder room, walk-in closet and private dining area.

Dining choices include the Hana Lounge and Bar for casual dining or the Pangaea Restaurant and Private Dining Room, with its use of fresh exotic ingredients, prepared in the finest tradition of European artistry.

The Westin Century Plaza Hotel and Tower

The Westin Century Plaza Hotel and Tower
2025 Avenue of the Stars
Los Angles, CA 90067
800-WESTIN-1
(310) 277-2000

Room Rates: $135–$280
Pet Charges or Deposits: $15 per day and $50 nonrefundable deposit.
Rated: 4 Paws 🐾🐾🐾🐾 1,072 rooms and suites with ocean and city views, wet bars, stocked refrigerators, twice daily maid service, 24-hour concierge and room service, laundry and valet service, complimentary Town Car service, international business center, pool, guest passes for the Century Plaza Spectrum Club and the Century City Tennis Club, multilingual staff.

A djacent to Beverly Hills, in the heart of the fashionable Westside of Los Angeles and minutes from major attractions is The Westin Century Plaza Hotel and Tower. Here you'll find spacious, accommodations with private lanais or balconies, magnificent views and amenities galore.

Whether in town on business or pleasure, travelers will appreciate the opportunity to relax by the garden swimming pool, work out the stresses of the day at one of the poolside fitness centers or take a relaxing stroll among the acres of lush gardens with the dog.

For a diversion from the ordinary dining fare, the Terrace il ristorante features Mediterranean cuisine fused with a Northern Italian flair. The Café Plaza offers casual indoor or outdoor dining for any meal of the day.

Residence Inn by Marriott

Residence Inn by Marriott
1700 North Sepulveda Boulevard
Manhattan Beach, CA 90266
800-331-3131
(310) 546-7627

Room Rates:	$99–$198, including complimentary breakfast buffet, AAA, AARP, Entertainment and Quest discounts.
Pet Charges or Deposits:	$8 per day and $75–$100 deposit/cleaning fee; small pets only; manager's approval required.
Rated: 3 Paws ❖ ❖ ❖	Oversized suites with fully equipped kitchens, pool, Jacuzzi, exercise room, Sport Court, laundry facilities, meeting facilities, business services, room service, manager-hosted evening hospitality.

Whether traveling on business or pleasure, the Residence Inn by Marriott is the next best thing to being home. The spacious 176 rooms and suites provide you with all the comforts and conveniences you'll need, including fully equipped kitchen, large living room, fireplace, private entrance, efficient work space with computer hookup, multi-phone lines and laundry facilities.

Start your day off at the Gatehouse with a complimentary continental breakfast, then move on to the fitness facilities for a workout before heading off for your business conference in one of the executive meeting rooms or a day of sightseeing. Your dog will love the landscaped grounds and the canine exercise areas. For that extra homey touch, guests are treated to a weekly manager's social hour and barbecue.

Colorado River Inn – Best Western

Colorado River Inn – Best Western
2371 West Broadway
Needles, CA 92363
800-528-1234
(760) 326-4552

Room Rates: $40–$65, AAA and AARP discounts.
Pet Charges or Deposits: $10 plus $20 deposit.
Rated: 3 Paws 🐾🐾🐾   63 rooms, some with refrigerators and microwaves, heated
                       indoor pool, sauna and whirlpool.

When looking for a desert oasis set among palm trees, the Colorado River Inn – Best Western has 63 comfortable rooms from which to choose, some with microwaves and refrigerators. Guests may opt to refresh themselves in the indoor heated swimming pool or relax in the sauna or whirlpool.

Located between Barstow and Kingman, Arizona, near the Colorado River, the inn's location is convenient to water skiing, wind surfing and swimming. There is plenty of room for you and your pet to get your daily exercise, not only surrounding the inn, but along the riverbank, too. If you like to gamble, the Laughlin Casinos are only 25 minutes from the inn.

Hyatt Newporter

Hyatt Newporter
1107 Jamboree Road
Newport Beach, CA 92660
800-233-1234
(714) 729-1234

Room Rates:	$155 and up, AAA discount.
Pet Charges or Deposits:	$50; pets up to 50 lbs.
Rated: 4 Paws 🐾🐾🐾🐾	410 rooms and 17 suites, plus 4 private villas with private pools and fireplaces, tennis courts, 9-hole golf course, 3 pools, 3 spas, health club, jogging and bicycling trails, business center, secretarial services, laundry, beauty salon and dress shop, restaurants and lounges, dog runs and exercise areas, near major attractions.

S et on 26 acres of plush gardens, the Hyatt Newporter overlooks the bay of Newport Beach. Enjoy the panoramic view of the bay from your balcony as the fresh sea air washes over you. At this luxury resort, guests may relax by one of the heated pools, play tennis or a few rounds of golf, jog or bike on the trails or visit the health club. Take some time out for a game of fetch with your dog at the beach or explore the lush gardens of this 26-acre paradise. If amusement parks are for you, you will appreciate the convenient proximity to major area attractions.

The casual atmosphere of the hotel's Jamboree Café features American classic cuisine while Italian dishes are in store at Ristorante Cantori. Join other guests for cocktails, fun and conversation at the Lobby Bar. Duke's Country Western Saloon is perfect for country dancing and live music.

Ojai Valley Inn

Ojai Valley Inn
Country Club Road
Ojai, CA 93023
800-422-6524
(805) 646-5511

Room Rates:	$99–$189, AAA discounts and packages available.
Pet Charges or Deposits:	$25 per day.
Rated: 4 Paws 🐾🐾🐾🐾	207 deluxe rooms and suites with balconies or patios, fireplaces and mini bars, 18-hole golf course, tennis courts, 2 pools, fitness center, whirlpool, steam rooms and saunas, conference rooms, horseback riding, petting farm.

Nestled on 220 enchanted acres is the mountain resort of Ojai Valley Inn. Built in 1923 in traditional Spanish style as a golf clubhouse, the building is now the focal point of the new and updated inn. The stunning setting fosters relaxation, inspiration, exhilaration, adventure and romance.

There are activities for all ages: a children's petting farm and Camp Ojai program, tennis courts, an 18-hole championship golf course, horseback riding, biking, hiking, swimming and an exercise area for the dog.

For real relaxation, try the 31,000-square-foot luxury spa facilities, where you will be pampered with a facial or massage or relax in one of the steam rooms or whirlpools. The art studio is a wonderful place for self-discovery, or if you prefer, relax and meditate in the beautiful wooded landscape surrounding the village plaza.

When it comes to fine dining, Chef Rex Hale offers California Coastal Harvest cuisine in the Vista Dining Room or visit The Oak Grill and Terrace, Splashes or the Club Bar for casual dining.

Residence Inn by Marriott

Residence Inn by Marriott
2025 Convention Center Way
Ontario, CA 91764
800-331-3131
(909) 983-6788

Room Rates:	$119–$149, including breakfast buffet, AAA and AARP discounts.
Pet Charges or Deposits:	$6 per day, a $50 cleaning fee and a $300 refundable deposit.
Rated: 3 Paws 🐾🐾🐾	200 rooms and suites with fully equipped kitchens and some fireplaces, heated swimming pool, whirlpool, Sport Court, health club privileges, meeting facilities, complimentary dog bowls, complimentary evening beverage.

I f you're looking for that "at home" feeling, that's the trademark of Residence Inn by Marriott. Whether you choose an oversized studio or a two-bed penthouse suite, the professional staff knows how to make you feel welcome. All accommodations offer a fully equipped kitchen, microwave and separate living and sleeping areas. Upon check-in, your dog will receive bowls with the inn's logo to make their stay more comfortable.

Guests will appreciate the complimentary grocery shopping service, satellite television, laundry facilities, valet service, curbside parking and more. After a hard day at work or play, unwind with a game of basketball or tennis on the Sport Court, take a dip in the heated pool or relax in the whirlpool. The landscaped grounds invite a stroll with your dog. The evening hospitality hour, weekly manager's barbecue and neighborhood setting will make you feel right at home.

The Estrella Inn at Palm Springs

The Estrella Inn at Palm Springs
415 South Belardo Road
Palm Springs, CA 92262
800-237-3687
(760) 320-4117

Room Rates:	$125–$275, AAA, AARP, Entertainment and Quest discounts.
Pet Charges or Deposits:	$20 and credit card deposit; limitations on certain breeds. Call for approval.
Rated: 4 Paws 🐾🐾🐾🐾	Guest rooms, suites and bungalows, daily California breakfast, three pools and two spas, outdoor barbecues, shuffleboard and volleyball courts, golf and tennis arrangements.

T he Estrella Inn is a desert hideaway that is still one of Palm Springs best kept secrets, but with $4 million in restorations, the cat will soon be out of the bag no doubt. Built in the 1930s and once host to stars of Hollywood's golden era, the entire inn has been remodeled. Most rooms are adorned with antiques and unusual beds and one-of-a-kind pieces while others boast a desert feel with Southwestern tile and embellishments, and still others with a roaring '20s theme. The bungalows have fireplaces and full kitchens. Suites are equipped with kitchenettes and guest rooms have wet bars and refrigerators. All guest quarters have balconies, patios or poolside views.

Outside, three acres of land are separated into three special environments, each with a pool: a rose garden, a fountain court and an original area maintained since the mid-'30s. There's even a pet exercise area.

The inn is in the heart of historic Palm Springs "village," just one block from famous Palm Canyon Drive and within walking distance of restaurants, bistros, boutiques and art galleries.

"Place in the Sun" Garden Hotel

"Place in the Sun" Garden Hotel
754 San Lorenzo
Palm Springs, CA 92264
800-779-2254
(760) 325-0254

Room Rates:	$49–$159, AAA, AARP and AKC discounts.
Pet Charges or Deposits:	$10 per day; small pets only.
Rated: 3 Paws 🐾🐾🐾	16 bungalows with garden patios or courtyards with barbecues, air-conditioning, fully equipped kitchens, swimming pool, whirlpool, putting green, conference room.

R esting on an acre of lush lawns and spacious gardens in the heart of Palm Springs, the "Place in the Sun" Garden Hotel offers guests personal hospitality for a luxurious yet casual vacation. The single-story studio and one-bedroom bungalows accommodate up to four guests and offer a living room, equipped kitchen, telephone and television. Add to that exceptional mountain views, landscaped private patios, courtyards, pool and barbecue.

The grounds, dotted with fruit trees and adjacent to a riverbed provide, you and your pet a scenic place to explore.

Riviera Resort and Racquet Club

Riviera Resort and Racquet Club
1600 North Indian Canyon Drive
Palm Springs, CA 92262
800-444-8311
(760) 327-8311

Room Rates:	$99–$850, AAA discounts.
Pet Charges or Deposits:	$300 deposit.
Rated: 4 Paws 😺😺😺😺	476 deluxe rooms and 36 luxury suites, all with refrigerators, microwaves and coffee makers, 5 rooms with private outdoor hydrotherapy pools, 2 heated pools, wading pool, exercise room, basketball and volleyball courts, lighted putting green, tennis courts, croquet, business and meeting facilities, data ports, valet laundry, restaurant.

Surrounded by mountains and drenched by the Southern California sun, the Palm Springs Riviera Resort and Racquet Club offers deluxe rooms and luxury suites, all with oversized beds, individual climate control and in-room movies. The staff promises to lavish you and your pet with prompt, courteous service.

Guests may linger poolside, tone up in the fitness center, relax with a massage, try a friendly game of croquet, perfect your stroke on the putting course, join in a game of basketball or volleyball or play a few games of tennis, day or night on the lighted courts. To get a bird's-eye view of the scenic area, take a ride of the famous aerial tram. The spacious grounds offer plenty of opportunity for you and your pet to explore the desert setting.

The Grill at the resort features poolside cuisine for lunch and dinner, with live evening entertainment on weekends.

Oxford Suites Resort

Oxford Suites Resort
631 Five Cities Drive
Pismo Beach, CA 93449
800-982-7848
(818) 773-3773

Room Rates:	$69–$89, full breakfast included, AAA, AARP, ABA and AKC discounts.
Pet Charges or Deposits:	$6 per day
Rated: 3 Paws 🐾🐾🐾	133 suites with microwaves, refrigerators, VCRs, large work areas, putting green, heated pool, wading pool, guest laundry, valet services, business services, conference facilities, convenience shop, video rentals, complimentary evening reception.

S et in the charming seaside village of Pismo Beach, the Oxford Suites Resort is known for comfort and convenience. Guests will appreciate the in-room microwaves and refrigerators and separate sleeping areas in the executive-king or family suites.

Start the morning with the complimentary breakfast buffet. After that, you may enjoy the resort's spa, pool or putting green or strike out on your own adventures. You and your dog might enjoy taking a walk around the landscaped grounds or resting under the shade trees in the courtyard.

After a busy day, top off the evening with the manager's complimentary evening reception with beverages and light hors d'oeuvres.

Spyglass Inn

Spyglass Inn
2705 Spyglass Drive
Pismo Beach, CA 93449
800-824-2612
(805) 773-4855

Room Rates: $59–$139, AAA and AARP discounts.
Pet Charges or Deposits: $10 per day; designated rooms only.
Rated: 3 Paws 🐾🐾🐾 82 comfortable rooms and suites, many with ocean views, some with kitchens, miniature golf, shuffleboard, heated pool, whirlpool, restaurant and lounge, near beaches, wineries and Hearst Castle.

Designed for comfort and enjoyment, the oceanfront Spyglass Inn offers guests freshly decorated rooms, many with views of the dramatic coastline, set amidst meticulously landscaped grounds. This quiet refuge beckons relaxation. Take a walk on the beach with your dog and drink in the beauty of the ever-changing tides, swim in the heated pool, soak your cares away in the spa, play a few rounds of miniature golf or a game of shuffleboard before heading out for an afternoon of sightseeing, wine tasting, fishing, sailing or other water sports.

For dining, the nautical theme of the Spyglass Inn Restaurant is carried out on an oceanfront deck where guests may sit and watch the sun seemingly sink into the ocean while enjoying a cocktail before dinner. Live entertainment is offered nightly.

Sheraton Suites Fairplex

Sheraton Suites Fairplex
601 W. McKinley Avenue
Pomona, CA 91768
800-722-4055
(909) 622-2220

Room Rates:	$105–$115, corporate, group, AAA, AARP and AKC discounts.
Pet Charges or Deposits:	$10 per day and $75 deposit.
Rated: 3 Paws 🐾🐾🐾	247 full-size suites, business center, fitness center, sauna, pool, spa, gift shop, airport shuttle, dog exercise area, near major attractions.

Situated on 487 acres with on-site business center, in-room computer hookups, meeting room and banquet facilities, the Sheraton Suites Fairplex is the first all-suites hotel in San Diego. The full-size, spacious suites provide guests with a living room and separate bedroom area, plus the conveniences of a microwave, wet bar and refrigerator.

Start your day with the complimentary full breakfast buffet before heading out for the fitness facilities for a workout or relax in the sauna or pool. Once you and your pet have explored the landscaped grounds, head across the street for a good run in the neighborhood park.

For your dining pleasure, the Sheraton offers gourmet dining at the Brass Ring Restaurant and nightly entertainment at Banner's Lounge.

The Westin Mission Hills Resort

The Westin Mission Hills Resort
71333 Dinah Shore Drive
Rancho Mirage, CA 92270
800-WESTIN-1
(760) 328-5955

Room Rates:	$150 and up, AAA discount and packages available.
Pet Charges or Deposits:	$100 deposit; small pets only.
Rated: 4 Paws 🐾🐾🐾🐾	512 rooms with balcony or patio, honor bar, in-room safe, attractive grounds, 3 pools, steam rooms, water slide, children's program, whirlpool, exercise room, croquet, soccer and softball field, volleyball court, 36 holes of golf, tennis courts, business and conference facilities, valet laundry, restaurant.

Deemed "The Playground of the Presidents," The Westin Mission Hills Resort brings the magic of the desert to life. This award-winning, four-star resort offers elegantly appointed rooms with balcony or patio, majestic waterfalls and warm desert breezes.

Choose from a variety of activities: Play tennis on one of the seven lighted courts or take a private lesson; tee off on one of the championship golf courses; play croquet, soccer or softball; or work out in the exercise room before having a relaxing massage or steam. Young guests will love the nature walks and "Catcus Kids" group activities. At the end of the day, take a walk with your dog around the landscaped grounds. You'll discover why this is a true desert oasis.

For your dining pleasure, the Bella Vista Restaurant has a wonderfully varied menu. Then follow up your feast with some chilled champagne and delectable chocolate-covered strawberries.

Fess Parker's Doubletree Resort

Fess Parker's Doubletree Resort
633 East Cabrillo Boulevard
Santa Barbara, CA 93103
800-879-2929
(805) 654-4333

Room Rates:	$229 and up, AAA, AARP, AKC and ABA discounts.
Pet Charges or Deposits:	$50 deposit.
Rated: 4 Paws 🐾🐾🐾🐾	360 luxury rooms with balcony or patio, in-room honor bar, coffee makers, putting green, pool, sauna, whirlpool, tennis courts, exercise room, shuffleboard and basketball court, data ports, conference facilities, airport transportation, 24-hour room service, coffee shop, cocktail lounge, spacious landscaped grounds, located across from the beach.

L ocated on the beautiful Santa Barbara coastline is Fess Parker's 25-acre resort. Here guests will find a coastal paradise, featuring 360 luxury guest rooms with amenities such as mini-bars, large bathrooms, 24-hour room service, a patio or balcony with a view of the ocean or the majestic Santa Ynez Mountains.

For fine dining, try the Café Los Arcos or Maxi's, both offering California cuisine brimming with fresh seafood.

Indulge yourself in beach activities, such as swimming, volleyball and sailing, all just steps from the resort. In addition to the beach, there's also an exercise area for dogs on-site.

Four Seasons Biltmore

Four Seasons Biltmore
1260 Channel Drive
Santa Barbara, CA 93108
800-332-3442
(805) 969-2261

Room Rates: $199 and up.
Pet Charges or Deposits: None.
Rated: 5 Paws ❀❀❀❀❀ 234 luxury oceanfront rooms and suites, with private bar, in-
                        room safes, 24-hour room service, multilingual concierge,
                        twice daily maid service, laundry and dry cleaning service,
                        video library, beauty salon, business center, restaurants and
                        cocktail lounge.

S anta Barbara is known for its sun-drenched oceanfront of celebrity estates, terraced vineyards, mountain canyons and sandy beaches overlooked by coastal bluffs. In the '20s, a copper baron claimed 20 acres of Pacific-front paradise for his lavish residence. Since then, it has been reborn as an adobe and terra cotta hotel flanked by private cottages known as the Santa Barbara Biltmore.

The dramatic landscape and amenable climate, backdrops for luxury guest rooms and suites and a cluster of guest cottages, have made this classic estate a popular retreat for celebrities and dignitaries for years.

Your pet will receive a four-star welcome at check-in with complimentary dog bowl with snacks and a special toy. The spacious grounds, beach and nearby park offer several places to explore. Pet sitters are available upon request.

San Ysidro Ranch of Santa Barbara

San Ysidro Ranch of Santa Barbara
900 San Ysidro Lane
Montecito, CA 93108
800-368-6788
(805) 969-5046

Room Rates:	$195–$700
Pet Charges or Deposits:	$75 cleaning fee; horses welcome; Privileged Pet Program.
Rated: 5 Paws 🐾🐾🐾🐾🐾	39 luxury room and suites, 21 cottages with private terraces, fireplaces and ocean views, health club facilities, tennis courts, restaurant, pub, dog runs and exercise areas, near major attractions.

Situated on 500 acres in the foothills of the Santa Ynez Mountains, the San Ysidro Ranch for more than a century has offered guests rustic, elegant accommodations in a country setting, blending the charm of yesterday with the tastes of today. Here you can roam colorful flower gardens, swim in the ocean-view pool, join in a friendly tennis match, try your hand at lawn bowling or pamper yourself with a therapeutic massage, facial or body wrap at the spa.

Animals love the "Privileged Pet Program." They receive complimentary dog bowls, dog cookies and bagels, bottled water, a dog bed and turn-down service with a dog bone every evening. There are dog runs and exercise areas plus 500 acres of oceanfront property to explore. After only one visit you and your pet will know why many guests throughout the years have called this their favorite retreat.

La Quinta Inn

La Quinta Inn
205 East Hospitality Lane
San Bernardino, CA 95814
800-687-6667
(909) 888-7571

Room Rates: $47–$59, including light breakfast, AAA and AARP discounts.
Pet Charges or Deposits: None; credit card imprint only.
Rated: 3 Paws ❖❖❖   153 rooms, cable television, movies on demand, outdoor
                         heated pool, fitness club privileges.

Located near ski areas, Lake Arrowhead, California State University, Loma Linda University and Medical Center and the Civic Light Opera is the San Bernardino – La Quinta Inn. The inn has a new look that goes beyond the crisp white exteriors and new landscaping to bigger rooms, oversized desks and data ports, comfy recliners and colorful decor.

Start the day with the complimentary Light Breakfast, featuring your choice of cereal, fresh fruit, bagels, pastries, juice, milk and coffee.

Top off your busy day at the pool, take advantage of fitness club privileges or enjoy a stroll through the groomed grounds with your pooch.

Carmel Highland – Doubletree Resort

Carmel Highland – Doubletree Resort
14455 Penasquitos Drive
San Diego, CA 92129
800-222-TREE
(760) 672-9100

Room Rates:	$94-$109, AAA, AARP, AKC and ABA discounts.
Pet Charges or Deposits:	$150 deposit; small pets only.
Rated: 3 Paws 🐾🐾🐾	172 rooms and suites with honor bar, coffee maker, cable television, meeting rooms, putting green, 18-hole golf course, 2 heated pools, sauna, whirlpool, lighted tennis courts, exercise room, restaurant, coffee shop, cocktail lounge.

At the San Diego Carmel Highland – Doubletree Resort, guests may choose from 172 rooms and suites, each with a patio or balcony view overlooking the 6,500-yard golf course. Improve your golf or tennis game with private or group instruction, work out in the 5,500-square-foot health and fitness center with lap pool, unwind with a massage or relax in the steam room or sauna.

For meals, the resort has three distinctive dining experiences. Trents offers regional continental cuisine in a quiet, intimate setting. Try the Terraces Café any time of the day and enjoy the indoor and outdoor seating overlooking the golf course. For a sports lounge atmosphere, don't miss the Club Double Eagle Club with music and nightly dancing.

Hanalei Hotel – Best Western

Hanalei Hotel – Best Western
2270 Hotel Circle North
San Diego, CA 92108
800-882-0858
(619) 297-1101

Room Rates:	$79–$160, AAA, AARP and AKC discounts.
Pet Charges or Deposits:	$50 deposit
Rated: 3 Paws 🐾🐾🐾	400 rooms and 12 suites with Polynesian atmosphere, pool and whirlpool, restaurant and coffee shop, conference facilities, close to major attractions.

E scape to a Hawaiian paradise right in the heart of San Diego at the Hanalei Hotel. Surrounded by lush landscape, spend your day relaxing on your private lanai or sun yourself by the inviting crystalline pool.

You and your dog will appreciate the tropical setting, with plenty of open space to explore before you take in one of the many local attractions or head out for a day of sightseeing.

The Hanalei is home to the Islands Restaurant, serving Hawaiian, Oriental and American cuisine. For lighter, more casual dining, there's the Peacock cafe. The Islands Lounge is perfect for an exotic drink, dancing and entertainment.

During the summer, enjoy a sumptuous feast and an authentic Hawaiian show. You'll find excellent golf courses and complete health facilities nearby. Also only minutes away are Sea World, the San Diego Zoo, Old Town, San Diego Mission de Acala and famed shopping areas.

Hilton Beach and Tennis Resort

Hilton Beach and Tennis Resort
1775 East Mission Bay Drive
San Diego, CA 92109
800-HILTONS
(619) 276-4010

Room Rates: $135–$235, AAA, AARP, AKC and ABA discounts.
Pet Charges or Deposits: $50 deposit.
Rated: 4 Paws 🐾🐾🐾🐾 357 rooms and suites with panoramic views, refrigerators,
                     mini-bars, coffee makers, 60 channel "on command" in-room
                     movie system, children's recreation program, heated pool,
                     sauna, whirlpools, wading pool, beach access, putting green,
                     conference facilities, laundry facilities, airport transportation,
                     18 acres of Mediterranean landscaped grounds.

O verlooking the Mission Bay, the San Diego Hilton Beach and Tennis Resort is set on 18 tropical acres. This exotic, Mediterranean vision offers guests panoramic views of the bay, with amenities such as mini-bars, coffee makers, a 60-channel movie system and refrigerators.

For dining, choose the casual atmosphere of Café Picante, serving breakfast, lunch and dinner, or the Banana Cabana that offers poolside snacks and light meals. For dinner, try Cavatappi's Italian cuisine or take in the sunset from the terrace at Fundidos, which offers live entertainment as well.

Guests may choose from recreational activities such as swimming, beach-combing, scuba diving, water skiing, windsurfing, boating, canoeing, paddleboating, bicycling or jogging. There also are tennis tournaments, health club facilities and a private dock. For the truly indulgent, spend a day at the full-service spa, where you will be pampered with facials, massage therapy, manicures and pedicures.

For your pet, there are 18 acres of land and beachfront to explore.

Holiday Inn — South Bay

Holiday Inn — South Bay
700 National City Boulevard
National City, CA 91950
800-HOLIDAY
(619) 474-2800

Room Rates:	$55, AAA and AARP discounts.
Pet Charges or Deposits:	$25 deposit; limit two pets per room.
Rated: 3 Paws 🐾🐾🐾	180 rooms, some with bay views, meeting rooms, data ports, outdoor pool and spa, valet service, airport transportation, full service restaurant, cocktail lounge with live entertainment.

C entrally located near major Southern California attractions just off of Interstate 5, the South Bay Holiday Inn offers guests deluxe rooms, including nonsmoking and handicap accommodations. Plus youths under 18 stay free with parents. Amenities include Spectravision movies and concierge service.

After a day of sightseeing and local attractions, guests can enjoy the heated pool or whirlpool. Business travelers will appreciate the conference and banquet facilities, featuring more than 6,000 square feet of meeting space for groups up to 300 people.

The South Bay Cafe serves breakfast, lunch and dinner while the South Bay Cantina offers cocktails.

La Quinta Inn

La Quinta Inn
10185 Paseo Montril
San Diego, CA 92129
800-531-5900
(619) 484-8800

Room Rates:	$45–$56, including light breakfast, AAA and AARP discounts.
Pet Charges or Deposits:	None; Credit card imprint only.
Rated: 3 Paws 🐾🐾🐾	120 rooms with refrigerators, large work areas with data ports, heated pool, landscaped grounds, near major attractions.

With Sea World and the San Diego Zoo nearby, San Diego's La Quinta Inn is a bargain for families on a budget. In addition to its proximity to major Southern California businesses and attractions, the inn offers spacious rooms, oversized bathrooms and large work areas.

Start your day with the complimentary Light Breakfast, with your choice of cereal, fresh fruit, bagels, pastries, juice, milk and coffee.

There's an exercise area on site, too, for your pet.

Marriott Hotel and Marina

Marriott Hotel and Marina
333 W. Harbor Drive
San Diego, CA 92101-7700
800-228-9290
(619) 234-1500

Room Rates:	$165–$225, AAA, AARP and AKC members.
Pet Charges or Deposits:	None; credit card imprint only.
Rated: 4 Paws 🐾🐾🐾🐾	1,355 rooms and suites with harbor views, 2 heated pools, sauna, whirlpools, health club, tennis courts, marina, conference facilities, restaurants, coffee shop and lounge, gift shops, hair salon, room service, laundry and dry cleaning, near major attractions, Honored Guest Program.

The dockside ambiance and resort setting of the San Diego Marriott Hotel and Marina invite you to indulge yourself. Whether visiting for business or pleasure, you'll enjoy the spacious guest rooms and stunning views of the harbor and the 446-slip marina.

Guests may spend time working out at the health club, playing tennis, sailing the harbor, enjoying a leisurely bike ride, jogging with the dog, sunning by the pool or relaxing in the sauna or hydrotherapy pools.

When mealtime arrives, there's The Sea Grill's fresh seafood selections; Las Cascadas or the Yacht Club, both featuring American favorites; Molly's for specialty dining; the more casual fare of Rudi's Bakeshop; and for appetizers and libations, D.W.'s Pub and the Lobby Lounge.

Mission Valley – Doubletree Hotel

Mission Valley – Doubletree Hotel
7450 Hazard Center Drive
San Diego, CA 92108
800-222-TREE
(619) 297-5466

Room Rates: $89, AAA and AARP discounts.
Pet Charges or Deposits: Credit card imprint as deposit.
Rated: 3 Paws 🐾🐾🐾 300 rooms and suites, 2 pools, sauna, whirlpool, tennis courts, exercise room, valet laundry, conference facilities, restaurant and lounge.

W hen it comes to California dreaming, one of the best places to wile away your day might just be the Doubletree Hotel, mere minutes from shopping, beaches and Southern California attractions. Guests are welcomed with Doubletree's signature greeting of freshly baked chocolate chip cookies. You may wish to spend the day pampering yourself in the spa or indoor/outdoor pools, playing tennis or working off those tasty cookies at the fitness center. Busy executives will appreciate the in-room data ports, mini-bar, room service, laundry and valet services. You and your pet are sure to enjoy the trails along the riverbank adjacent to the hotel.

Diners may choose from the causal dining at the Fountain Café or heat up the night with entertainment, dinner and dancing at Club Max before topping off the evening with a nightcap at Windows Lobby Bar.

Mission Valley Hilton

Mission Valley Hilton
901 Camino Del Rio South
San Diego, CA 92108
800-733-2332
(619) 543-9000

Room Rates:	$109, AAA and AARP discounts.
Pet Charges or Deposits:	$25 fee.
Rated: 3 Paws 🐾🐾🐾	350 rooms, coffee maker, fully stocked armoire cafes, in-room movies, heated pool with poolside food service, spa and dry sauna, exercise room, health club nearby, valet laundry service, covered parking.

Simply put, the luxurious, award-winning accommodations of the San Diego-Mission Valley Hilton will impress you. From the spacious rooms with their overstuffed upholstered chairs, cheerful lighting, and comfortable beds, to the remote-control cable televisions and two in-room telephones, you will appreciate all of the effort put into these welcoming touches.

Once you're settled into your room, take advantage of the heated pool for a relaxing diversion or work out at the full-service health club located nearby and then wind down in the dry sauna.

The two on-site restaurants provide a choice of fine and fun dining. Choose the Monterey Whaling Company for any meal. The menu features a daily variety of fresh fish, pasta, salads and steaks. The adjacent Pub offers the latest sports action on 11 television monitors to enjoy with your complimentary happy hour hors d'oeuvres and libations.

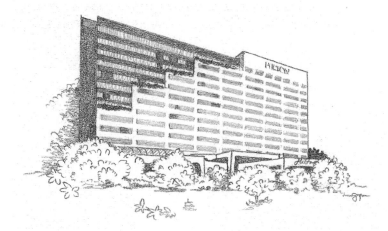

Princess Resort

Princess Resort
1404 West Vacation Road
San Diego, CA 92109
800-344-2626
(619) 274-4630

Room Rates:	$140–$355, AAA discount.
Pet Charges or Deposits:	None
Rated: 3 Paws ❖ ❖ ❖	462 rooms and bungalows with refrigerators and coffee makers, 5 pools, sauna, whirlpool, 18-hole putting course, lighted tennis courts, marina, health club, recreational program, canoeing, paddleboats, bicycles, conference facilities, secretarial services.

I f you ever dreamed of vacationing on a tropical island, then the San Diego Princess Resort might just be a dream come true. Located in the heart of San Diego's Mission Bay, this island resort is in a world of its own. The exotic setting is ablaze with color, sparkling waterfalls, winding lagoons and pathways weaving throughout the island for you and your dog to explore. The 462 single-story guest rooms and suites offer comfort and panoramic views, making this an ideal place for an exotic family weekend, a romantic getaway or business meeting.

Guests may practice their putt on the 18-hole putting links; work out at the fitness center; tour the island by bicycle; jog on the 1.3-mile course; play video games, tennis, croquet, volleyball or shuffleboard; swim; sail; or relax with a sauna and massage.

For dining, try the family-style Village Café, the casual elegance of Dockside, dine poolside at Tropics or enjoy the live entertainment at Barefoot Bar and Grill.

Residence Inn by Marriott – Rancho Bernardo

Residence Inn by Marriott – Rancho Bernardo
11002 Rancho Carmel Drive
San Diego, CA 92128
800-331-3131
(619) 673-1900

Room Rates:	$129–$179, including breakfast buffet, AAA and AARP discounts.
Pet Charges or Deposits:	$6 per day and $50 nonrefundable deposit.
Rated: 3 Paws ❖❖❖	123 rooms and suites with separate living and sleeping areas, meeting rooms, heated pool, whirlpool, Sport Court, complimentary evening beverages.

When looking for relaxing and affordable accommodations with all the amenities of home, visit the San Diego-Rancho Bernardo – Residence Inn by Marriott. Here you will find comfortable, spacious rooms and suites with wood-burning fireplace, separate sleeping and living areas and grocery shopping service. During the week, there is a complimentary hospitality hour to make you will feel welcome.

Start your day with the breakfast buffet served at the Gatehouse, followed by a day of sightseeing and attractions or stay where you are and relax by the pool or venture to the Sport Court for a game of tennis, volleyball or basket ball. You and your dog can enjoy the landscaped grounds and exercise area.

Residence Inn by Marriott

Residence Inn by Marriott
5400 Kearny Mesa Road
San Diego. CA 92126
800-331-3131
(619) 278-2100

Room Rates:	$85–$135, including breakfast buffet, AAA and AARP discounts.
Pet Charges or Deposits:	$50 nonrefundable deposit
Rated: 3 Paws 🐾🐾🐾	144 rooms and suites with kitchens and some fireplaces, heated pool, whirlpool, Sport Court, health club privileges, meeting facilities, complimentary evening beverage, concierge services, pet bowls with inn's logo and exercise area for pets, near major attractions.

C onvenient to major Southern California attractions, San Diego's Residence Inn by Marriott dispels the myth that there's no place like home. When you have to be away from home on business or vacation, you will appreciate the inn's comforts and conveniences.

From the spacious accommodations, some with fireplaces, separate sleeping and living areas, fully equipped kitchens, laundry facilities, room service from any of the local restaurants, work areas and meeting facilities to the manager-hosted continental breakfast buffet and informal hospitality hour, you're bound to feel at home here.

For recreation, this retreat offers a heated pool, two whirlpools, three barbecue areas, Marriott's trademark Sport Court where you can play basketball, volleyball or tennis, landscaped grounds and an exercise area for your pet.

U.S. Grant Hotel

U.S. Grant Hotel
326 Broadway
San Diego, CA 92101
800-HERITAGE
(619) 232-3121

Room Rates:	$145 and up, AAA, AARP and AKC discounts.
Pet Charges or Deposits:	None
Rated: 4 Paws 🐾🐾🐾🐾	340 rooms and suites, antique furnishings, restaurant and cocktail lounge. "Pampered Pet Program" for dogs and cats.

Built in 1910 by Ulysses S. Grant Jr. in memory of his father, the 340 rooms and suites of the historic U.S. Grant Hotel have housed 12 visiting presidents. Exquisitely restored and listed with Preferred Hotels Worldwide, the hotel is known for its Queen Anne reproduction furniture, comfortable and spacious rooms and four-star amenities. For fine dining, you need look no further than the Grant Grill, winner of numerous awards for excellence. A companion lounge features a variety of cocktails.

Four-legged guests will enjoy the "Pampered Pet Program," where your cat will be offered a beckoning feast of warm milk, a scratching post, catnip and squeaky toys. Vacationing dogs will be indulged with soft pillows for naps, chef-prepared gourmet dinners, rawhide toys and turn-down service with a dog biscuit.

La Quinta Inn – Vista

La Quinta Inn – Vista
630 Sycamore Avenue
Vista, CA 92083-7910
800-531-5900
(760) 727-8180

Room Rates:	$47–$58, includes continental breakfast, AAA and AARP discounts.
Pet Charges or Deposits:	None; small pets only
Rated: 3 Paws 🐾🐾🐾	106 large rooms with spacious work areas with data ports, expanded bathrooms, laundry and dry cleaning service, heated outdoor pool, workout privileges, children stay free.

When looking for a place to unwind after a day of sightseeing or a hectic business meeting, the San Diego-Vista La Quinta Inn has everything you need. If you are traveling on business, the large rooms offer spacious work areas with data ports for your lap-top computer, 24-hour fax and message services, with meeting space for up to 45 people.

If you are in the Southern California area to take in the local attractions with your family, you will also appreciate the spacious Gold Medal rooms featuring fresh decor with expanded bathrooms and the daily continental breakfast. Plus kids stay free.

You and the family, including your dog, can play and explore at the nearby park. Just stop by the desk and ask for directions.

Capistrano Inn – Best Western

Capistrano Inn – Best Western
27174 Ortega Highway
San Juan Capistrano, CA 92675
800-441-9438
(714) 493-5661

Room Rates:	$65–$125, including breakfast weekdays, AAA and AARP discounts.
Pet Charges or Deposits:	None; small pets only.
Rated: 3 Paws 🐾🐾🐾	108 rooms, some with balconies, honor bars, microwaves and refrigerators, some efficiency kitchens, heated pool, whirlpool, complimentary evening beverages, meeting facilities, valet laundry.

Situated on a knoll overlooking picturesque Capistrano Valley is the Capistrano Inn – Best Western. Conveniently located near Mission San Juan Capistrano, Dana Point, the Pacific Ocean and major Southern California attractions, this charming inn offers guests comfortable rooms, some with balconies, a heated swimming pool and spa.

Stop by the desk and get directions to the nearby park where you and your dog can enjoy a game of fetch. At the end of your busy day, return to the inn for a free beverage at the complimentary happy hour.

Big America Hotel – Best Western

Big America Hotel – Best Western
1725 N. Broadway
Santa Maria, CA 93454
800-426-3213
(805) 922-5200

Room Rates:	$55–$90, including continental breakfast, AAA, AARP, AKC and ABA discounts.
Pet Charges or Deposits:	None; manager's approval required.
Rated: 3 Paws ❁❁❁	104 rooms and suites, in-room refrigerators, cable TV, heated pool, whirlpool, meeting and conference facilities, restaurant and lounge.

Midway between Los Angeles and the Central Coast in scenic Santa Maria is the Big America Hotel – Best Western. This hotel offers business travelers and vacationers comfortable rooms and family atmosphere at an affordable price.

Each of the guest rooms features a wet bar, deluxe bathroom with separate dressing area and large comfortable beds. Choose from 50 specially designed rooms with motifs reflecting each of the states from Alaska to Wyoming.

For aquatic leisure, the hotel offers a heated outdoor pool and whirlpool. Stop by the front desk for directions to a nearby park where you and your dog can stretch your legs.

Whether dining with a business associate or your family, check out the famous Strawberry Patch restaurant, featuring home-style cooking at popular prices.

Loews Santa Monica Beach Hotel

Loews Santa Monica Beach Hotel
1700 Ocean Avenue
Santa Monica, CA 90401
800-12-LOEWS
(310) 458-6700

Room Rates:	$245 and up, AAA and AARP discounts.
Pet Charges or Deposits:	$500 deposit per pet
Rated: 4 Paws 🐾🐾🐾🐾	350 deluxe rooms and suites, ocean views, twice daily maid service, valet laundry, conference and banquet facilities, business center, health club, heated indoor/outdoor pool, playground, childcare, restaurant, coffee shop, entertainment.

A five-story atrium of shimmering glass frames a panoramic view of the blue Pacific at Loews Santa Monica Beach Hotel. Guest rooms are a blend of California casual, with bleached rattan and wicker furniture in a palette of cool colors. The luxury suites offer living and dining areas, wet bar, outdoor patio, master bedroom and marble bathroom with Jacuzzi and skylight.

For dining, the Riva offers ocean views and Mediterranean-style seafood. For casual alfresco dining, try the Café or the Poolside Grill. The Lobby Bar and Lounge provide live entertainment nightly.

Venture down the private pathway from the hotel to the inviting golden sands where you and your pet can enjoy the sun and surf.

Kronberg Inn – Best Western

Kronberg Inn – Best Western
1440 Mission Drive
Solvang, CA 93463
800-528-1234
(805) 688-2383

Room Rates: $50–$100, AAA and AARP discounts.
Pet Charges or Deposits: $10 per day; small pets only; manager's approval required.
Rated: 3 Paws 🐾🐾🐾 39 large rooms with patio, refrigerator, continental breakfast, pool and spa.

T he Kronberg Inn is three blocks from the heart of the Danish community of Solvang and just 45 minutes from Santa Barbara.

This quaint Danish inn, with its traditional Tudor style architecture and pitched roofs, offers guests 39 deluxe rooms, decorated in charming country decor plus the convenience of in-room spa tub, refrigerator, in-room coffee and a patio or balcony. A complimentary continental breakfast kicks off the day.

It's guaranteed that you and your dog will enjoy the walk around town, exploring the quaint neighborhoods and shops.

Summit Travelodge

Summit Travelodge
500 Steuber Road
Tehachapi, CA 93561
800-578-7878
(805) 823-8000

Room Rates:	$49–$59, AAA and AARP discounts.
Pet Charges or Deposits:	None
Rated: 3 Paws 🐾🐾🐾	81 rooms, conference facilities, pool, Jacuzzi, on-site gas station, mini-mart and deli, Summit Dining Hall and Saloon.

The city of Tehachapi with an elevation of 4,000 feet has become a popular place for glider planes, sky diving and golf. Centrally located from Bakersfield, Mojave and Edwards Air Force Base, the Tehachapi Summit Travelodge it the place to stay when visiting the area on business or pleasure.

Try the hotel's Summit Dining Hall and Saloon for breakfast, lunch or dinner. Sample the Cowboy Sunrise for breakfast—sliced tri-tip, outlaw beans, skillet potatoes, two eggs, tortillas and salsa. The lunch menu offers a variety of sandwiches and burgers. For dinner, select from one of the many of mouthwatering steaks, oak-grilled chicken or ribs.

Your pet is bound to love the open space that surrounds the hotel.

Residence Inn by Marriott

Residence Inn by Marriott
3701 Torrance Boulevard
Torrance, CA 90503
800-331-3131
(310) 543-4566

Room Rates:	$145 and up, including breakfast buffet, AAA and AARP discounts.
Pet Charges or Deposits:	$6 per day, plus a $40-$60 deposit.
Rated: 3 Paws 🐾🐾🐾	247 rooms and suites, many with fireplaces, full kitchens, meeting facilities, heated pool, whirlpool, exercise room and Sport Court, complimentary evening beverages, Japanese suites and amenities.

When searching for spacious accommodations or a convenient location for a business meeting, look to the local Residence Inn by Marriott. Choose from a studio or a one- or two-bedroom suite, all with fireplaces and 50 percent more space than traditional hotel rooms. Enjoy the conveniences of valet service, laundry facilities, daily housekeeping and fully equipped kitchens. There is even a complimentary continental breakfast served daily at the Gatehouse and a weekly manager's barbecue and social hour to get to know your neighbors.

Your dog will appreciate the pet exercise area, where he'll have plenty of room to explore. When your day is over, relax with a swim or whirlpool or play basketball, racquetball or volleyball on the Sport Court.

For those guest who appreciate Japanese accommodations, there are suites available with slippers, rice bowls, chop sticks, miso soup, green tea, rice cookers, rice and information and brochures in Japanese. There is even an AT&T in-room translator available 24 hours a day.

Hilton Garden Inn at Six Flags

Hilton Garden Inn at Six Flags
27710 The Old Road
Valencia, CA 91355-1053
800-HILTONS
(805) 254-8800

Room Rates:	$89–$145, AAA, AARP, AKC and ABA discounts.
Pet Charges or Deposits:	$10 per day; small pets only.
Rated: 3 Paws 🐾🐾🐾	152 rooms, some with balconies, landscaped courtyard, business center, conference facilities, heated pool, whirlpool, exercise room, restaurant and cocktail lounge.

The Valencia Hilton Garden Inn at Six Flags offers guests comfortable, casual accommodations at an affordable price. Located minutes from major area attractions, the inn's oversized guest rooms feature vaulted ceilings, comfortable sitting areas and large work desks. For those needing conference space, the business center features four meeting rooms totaling 2,500 square feet of space.

With its Six Flags locale, guests who love theme parks will find this an extra convenient location. If your business keeps you closer to the inn, its recreational facilities will help you unwind from a busy day.

The whole family will enjoy the casual dining at the Great American Grill Restaurant that serves breakfast, lunch and dinner. End your day in the cozy lobby lounge.

La Quinta Inn

La Quinta Inn
5818 Valentine Road
Ventura, CA 93003
800-687-6667
(805) 658-6200

Room Rates:	$50–$57, including light breakfast, AAA and AARP discounts.
Pet Charges or Deposits:	None; single small pet only.
Rated: 3 Paws ❧ ❧ ❧	142 rooms, many with refrigerators, meeting facilities, heated pool, whirlpool, driving range and putting green.

The Ventura – La Quinta Inn offers families on vacation and business travelers the comfort and conveniences of home at a reasonable price. From the oversized bathrooms, the large work area with data port phones to the comfortable recliners and king-size beds in all rooms, the accommodations are suitable for a week or a weekend.

You and your dog will enjoy roaming the landscaped grounds, perfect for a morning stroll. Then continue your morning with the complimentary First Light breakfast, featuring your choice of cereals, fresh fruit, pastries, bagels, juice, milk and coffee before heading out for the day.

Hampton Inn

Hampton Inn
3145 E. Garvey North
West Covina, CA 91791
800-HAMPTON
(818) 967-5800

Room Rates:	$49–$69, includes continental breakfast, AAA, AARP and Lifestyle 50 discounts.
Pet Charges or Deposits:	None; no large pets.
Rated: 3 Paws 🐾🐾🐾	124 rooms and suites with work areas, modem hookups, valet services, health spa, hospitality and meeting rooms.

Located near major attractions and Cal Poly Pomona, the Hampton Inn offers friendly service and comfortable surroundings for business travelers and vacationers, from the hospitality and meeting rooms to the complimentary continental breakfast and morning paper.

If you love golf, there are several golf courses nearby, as well as tennis and racquetball courts. Guests may spend the day lounging by the pool, take advantage of the adjacent fitness center or head out for a day of sightseeing or excitement at one of the theme parks located only minutes away. When you add that your pets and children under 18 stay free, to the inn's guarantee of 100 percent satisfaction, what more do you need?

Le Montrose Suite Hotel De Gran Luxe

Le Montrose Suite Hotel De Gran Luxe
900 Hammond Street
West Hollywood, CA 90069
800-637-7200
(310) 855-1115

Room Rates:	$185–$475, AAA, AARP and AKC discounts.
Pet Charges or Deposits:	$250 deposit; pets up to 30 lbs.
Rated: 4 Paws 🐾🐾🐾🐾	125 suites with fireplace, refrigerator and kitchenette, meeting rooms, whirlpool, sauna, pool, tennis court, exercise room, restaurant, near major attractions.

Nestled in a quiet residential area one block east of Beverly Hills sits the Le Montrose Suite Hotel De Gran Luxe. This celebrity hideaway offers guests a departure from ordinary accommodations. Charming, comfortable suites feature a sunken living room, cozy fireplace, refrigerator, color TV with VCR, maid service and, for the business traveler, multi-line phone, data port, voice mail and in-suite fax.

The friendly staff and attention to detail will remind you of a fine European hotel. Guests may relax in the heated rooftop pool and spa, play tennis, work out in the fitness center or enjoy a massage. Diners may choose the rooftop terrace with its panoramic view or an intimate dinner at the Library Restaurant.

Southern California

Leashes are required unless otherwise stated.

ANAHEIM

Yorba Regiona Park is a popular, 166-acre park on La Palma Avenue off of Weir Canyon Road and Yorba Linda Boulevard. There is a small fee for parking. For more information, call (714) 970-1640.

BAKERSFIELD

Kern River County Park offers you and your dog a combination of mountains and meadows to explore. Located on Alfred Harrell Highway off of Panorama Drive. For more information, call (805) 861-2345.

Tule Elk State Reserve protects a herd of dwarf elks. It's 956 acres offer plenty of room to roam. There is a natural history display, visitors center, viewing area and a picnicking area. Located off of SR 119 and Tupman Road. For more information, call (805) 765-5004.

BEVERLY HILLS

Laurel Canyon Park is in Coldwater Canyon about 3 miles off of Mulholland Drive, before the fire station. Here you will find a leash-free paradise 6 a.m. to 10 a.m. and 3 p.m. to dusk. There are picnic tables and lots of shade trees. Even the rich and famous canines are known to come here from time to time. The park is equipped with water and pooper scoopers. For more information, call (818) 756-8190.

Will Rogers Memorial Park, across from the Beverly Hills Hotel on the corner of Canon and Beverly Drives at Sunset Boulevard, is in the center of posh Beverly Hills. It is a great place to burn off some energy after a day of shopping on Rodeo Drive. For more information, call (310) 285-2541.

BRIDGEPORT

Bodie State Historic Park consists of a 500 acre former mining town. There is enough open space for you and your dog to enjoy yourselves, if you don't mind the occasional ghost. Located off of Highway 270 and Bodie Road; follow the road east for 13 miles to reach the park. There are fees for your vehicle and your dog. For more information, call (619) 647-6445.

BURBANK

Woodley Park has a wonderful exercise course. It is a great park for a picnic with your dog. From Burbank, take Ventura Freeway 134 to Ventura Freeway 101. Travel westbound to San Diego 405 and take the Burbank Boulevard Exit. Make a right on Woodley Avenue. The park is on the right, past the Japanese Garden. For more information, call (818) 756-8190.

COSTA MESA

There are several neighborhood parks with plenty of running room.

Brentwood Park, 265 East Brentwood
Canyon Park, 970 Arbor Street
Del Mesa Park, 2080 Mainstee Drive
Estancia Park, 1900 Adams
Gisler Park, 1250 Gisler Street
Harper Park, 425 East 18th Street
Lions Park, 570 West 18th Street
Shiffer Park, 3134 Bear Street
Tanager Park, 1780 Hummingbird Drive
Vista Park, 1200 Victoria Street
Wakeham Park, 3400 Smalley Street
Wimbledon Park, 3440 Wimbledon Way

JOSHUA TREE

Joshua Tree National Park encompasses 870 square miles of California desert. It's north of Interstate 10 and east of Desert Hot Springs. Take Highway 60 to Interstate 10 and continue to Highway 62 northeast, approximately 39 miles to Twenty-nine Palms. The visitors center is on Utah Trail, south of Highway 62. There is an entrance fee. There is a wide variety of wildlife and fauna, including the desert bighorn and lots of Joshua trees. There are granite formations and mountains rising from the valley floors to about 3,000 feet above sea level. For more information, call (619) 367-7511.

LA JOLLA

There are miles of beachfront for you and your dog to explore at La Jolla Shores Beach, west of Camino del Oro. Dogs are only allowed on the beach before 9 a.m. and after 6 p.m. For more information, call (619) 221-8901.

LAKE ARROWHEAD – SAN BERNARDINO

Located in the town of Lake Arrowhead is the San Bernardino National Forest, a popular location for fishing and winter sports. For directions and more information, and restrictions, contact the Chamber of Commerce at (909) 336-1547.

Big Bear Lake is one of California's largest recreational areas, located about 30 miles northeast of San Bernardino. Here you and your pet may camp, picnic, go horseback riding, fishing and swimming in designated areas or snow skiing and sledding in the winter. Call (909) 866-7000 for more information.

LOMPOC

La Purisma Mission State Historic Park, a 966-acre park, is 4 miles northeast on Purisima Road off of Highway 1. Originally founded in 1787 as a mission, it was destroyed by the 1812 earthquake and rebuilt from 1813 to 1822. The park includes nine buildings and an historic aqueduct system. There are more than 12 miles of hiking and riding trails for you and your dog to explore. There is a small entrance fee. Call (805) 733-3713 for more information.

LOS ANGELES

Elysian Park is more than 550 acres with hilltop views of the city. Located between Interstate 5, Highway 101 and Highway 110, the park is accessed from the Stadium Way exit. Follow the signs to the park, then turn left on Elysian Park Drive. For more information, call (213) 226-1402.

Griffith Park has more than 4,000 acres to roam and hundreds of different species of trees to inspect. Bounded by Highway 101, Interstate 5 and Highway 134, the park is off of Interstae 5 at Los Feliz Boulevard. For more information, call (213) 665-5188.

Kenneth Hahn State Recreation Area, off of the Santa Monica Freeway at La Cienega Boulevard, is where the 1932 Olympics were held. There is a lovely lake and stream, plus lots of hiking trails for you and your dog to explore. For more information, call (213) 291-0199.

Santa Monica Mountains National Recreation Area has more than 65,000 acres of nature with everything from waterfalls, meadows and creeks to forests and beaches. The park runs from Beverly Hills to Ventura. Contact the ranger office for directions and more information at (818) 597-9192.

There are several neighborhood parks with plenty of running room:
Arroyo Seco Park, 5566 Via Marisol Street
Barnsdall Park, 4800 Hollywood Boulevard
City Hall Park, 200 North Main Street

Crestwood Hills Park, 1000 Hanley Avenue
Harold A. Henry Park, 890 South Lucerne Avenue
Hollenbeck Recreation Center, 415 South St. Louis Street
Holmby Park, 601 Club View Drive
Jim Gillam Recreation Center, South La Brea Avenue
Leimert Plaza, 4395 Leimert Boulevard
Lincoln Park Recreation Center, 3501 Valley Boulevard
Norman O. Houston Park, 4800 South La Brea Avenue
Northridge Park, 10058 Reseda Boulevard
Pershing Square Park, 532 South Olive Street
Silverlake Park, 1850 West Silverlake
South Park, 345 East 51st Street
Sycamore Grove Park, 4702 N. Figueroa Street
Temescal Canyon Park, 15900 Pacific Coast Highway
Westwood Recreation Center, 1350 Sepulveda Boulevard

NEEDLES

Jack Smith Park, at Interstate 40 and Park Moabi Road, is on the Colorado River. Here you and your pooch can spend the day lazing on the riverbanks and dipping your toes in the water.

Moabi Regional Park is 1,027 acres on the Colorado River. You can rent houseboats and explore the river or the desert region in surrounding the area. The entrance is at Interstate 40 and Park Moabi Road. There is a vehicle fee and a fee for your dog. For more information, call (619) 326-3831.

NEWPORT BEACH

Newport Harbor and Newport Dunes is probably one of the most scenic small harbors in the world. Your dog will love exploring the sand dunes. The harbor office is at 1901 Bayside Drive. For more information, call (714) 723-4511.

OJAI

Los Padres National Forest is in the Ojai Valley in the town of Goleta. The park is made up of 1,750,000 acres of pine trees, desert, coastal areas and a condor sanctuary. For more information, call (805) 683-6711.

Foster Park is 205 acres of open space, off of Highway 33, south of Ojai. For more information, call (805) 654-3951.

Libbey Park consists of 15 acres of oak trees. It is in downtown Ojai, across from the Arcade.

Soule Park, east of downtown Ojai on Boardman Road, is a beautiful county park.

PALM SPRINGS

Idyllwild County Park is 202 acres of open space, located at the north end of County Park Road, a mile off of Highway 243. There is an entrance fee for you and your dog.

Palm Springs Indian Canyons consists of three separate canyons to explore. This secluded area is off of South Palm Canyon Drive. For more information, call (619) 325-5673.

PISMO BEACH

The area was once known for the Pismo clam, but today butterflies reign as the local attraction from November to March as thousands of Monarchs fill the trees. The beach area lies off scenic U.S. 101. Entrance fees are paid at the Grand Avenue entrance, but there is no entry fee if you head west on Highway 1, park and walk in at Grand Avenue entrance. Here you and your pet will discover dunes to explore, beaches to comb and miles of trails to roam. For more information, call (805) 927-4509 or (805) 773-4382.

RANCHO MIRAGE

Salton Sea State Recreation Area is 234 feet below sea-level and is the largest inland body of water in the world. There are 16 miles of shoreline and five beaches to explore. Take Highway 111 southeast of Mecca to the visitors center on the west side of the highway. Call (619) 393-3502 for more information.

SAN BERNARDINO – see Lake Arrowhead

SAN DIEGO

Fiesta Island, a paradise for man and his best friend, is on Fiesta Island Road off of Interstate 5, Sea World Drive exit. Here you can enjoy a leashless romp in the surf or a walk on the beach enjoying the outstanding views of downtown San Diego and Mission Bay. So bring your picnic lunch and don't forget the ball. For more information, call (619) 221-8901.

Los Penasquitos Canyon Preserve, off of Interstate 15 on Black Mountain Road, offers groves of shady oak trees for a relaxing picnic. Then venture on to the creekside trails leading to the waterfalls and pools of water at the bottom of the canyon. In the spring there are magnificent fields of wildflowers to behold. For more information, call (619) 685-1350.

Mission Beach and Pacific Beach, on West Mission Bay Drive and Mission Park Boulevard, offer miles of coastline to enjoy, but dogs are limited to the hours before 9 a.m. or after 6 p.m.

Mission Trails Regional Park consists of 5,700 acres, making it the largest urban park in the United States. Hike up to Cowles Mountain for terrific summit views or make your way to the Old Mission Dam built by Native Americans. Located off of Interstate 8 at the College Avenue exit on Navajo Road. Park at Goldcrest Drive where the trail begins to Cowles Mountain. For more information, call (619) 533-4051.

Mount Woodson is a haven for rock climbers. This leashless refuge offers peace, serenity and georgeous views of the Pacific. Located off of Interstate 15 north of San Diego, the entrance is at the California Division of Forestry Fire Station off of Highway 67. For more information, call (619) 695-1400.

Ocean Beach Park is the most popular beach in the area for dog lovers. Referred to as "Dog Beach," the off-leash section at the north end of the beach will be your dog's favorite place to run. Take Interstate 5 to the Interstate 8 exit. Follow the signs to Sunset Cliffs Boulevard and bear right to reach the entrance. For more information, call (619) 221-8901.

Wooded Hill Nature Trail, off of Sunrise Highway, has the highest wooded summit in the Laguna Mountains. No leashes are required, allowing you and your dog a vigorous hike up the vista for a superb view of San Diego and Catalina Island. For more information, call (619) 445-6235.

SANTA BARBARA

There are several neighborhood parks with acres of running room:

Alameda Park, 1400 Santa Barbara Street
Mission Park, Laguna and Mission Drives
San Antonio Canyon Park, San Antonio Creek Road
Shoreline Park, Marina and Shoreline Drives

Arroyo Burro County Beach, 2981 Cliff Drive, west of Las Positas Road, is a wonderful place for you and your dog to chase some waves. It also has a small outdoor café where you and your dog can dine together. For more information, call (805) 963-7109.

Santa Barbara Botanic Gardens is 65 acres with more than 1,000 species of native California plants. Located on Mission Canyon Drive off of Foothill Road, this constantly blooming garden has more than 5 miles of trails to explore. There is an admission fee. Call (805) 563-2521 for more information.

SANTA MARIA

Adam Park, 600 West Enos Drive, has 30 acres of grass where you and your dog can play a game of Frisbee.

Preisker Park is a 40-acre park with a delightful pond full of ducks and geese. The Grandchildren's Grove has monarch butterflies in season. Located at 2301 North Broadway.

Waller Park, at South Broadway and Goodwin Road, is a wonderful park full of tall pine trees, a tranquil lake and room for your dog to exercise. For more information, call (805) 934-6211.

There are several neighborhood parks with acres of running room:

Alice Trefts Park, 510 E. Park Avenue
Armstrong Park, 1000 E. Chapel Street
Atkinson Park, 1000 N. Railroad Avenue
Buena Vista Park, 800 S. Pine Street
Central Plaza Park, 100 N. Broadway
Grogan Park, 1155 W. Rancho Verde
Joe White Park, 500 S. Pine Street
Maramonte Park, 620 E. Sunrise Drive
Memorial Park, 200 N. Pine Street
Oakley Park, 1300 N. Western Avenue
Rice Park, 700 E. Sunset Avenue
Russel Park, 1000 W. Church Street

SOLVANG

Hans Christian Andersen Park, off of Highway 246 at Atterdag Road, is a 52-acre park left in its natural, rugged state. A 164-foot-high waterfall cascades over the cliffs in the rainy season. There are trails to the falls, picnic areas, a ball field and volleyball court. Call 800-468-6765 for more information.

TEHACHAPI

Tehachapi Mountain Park has wonderful scenic trails for you and your dog to explore. Located off the Highway 202, exit south, head west and stay on Tucker Road until you reach Highline Road. Follow that for about 1½ miles, then turn left on Water Canyon Road and follow this road for two miles until you reach the park.

VENTURA

Grant Memorial Park has some wonderful views of the Channel Islands from the grassy knoll area. There is plenty of room to roam, but not much in the way of shade. Located two blocks east of Ventura Avenue on Ferro Drive.

PETS WELCOME!

National and State Parks and Beaches

CALIFORNIA'S PARKS, FORESTS, RECREATION AREAS, PRESERVES AND SEASHORE AREAS THAT ALLOW PETS

Please Note

Pets must be on leash at all times and may be restricted to certain areas. For directions, use fees, pet charges and general information contact the numbers listed below.

❖
NATIONAL PARKS
GENERAL INFORMATION

National Park Service
Fort Bragg, Building 201
Bay and Franklin streets
San Francisco, CA 94123
(415) 556-0560

❖
NATIONAL PARKS

Death Valley National Park
Superintendent's Office
Death Valley, CA 92328
(619) 786-2331

Joshua Tree National Park
Superintendent's Office
74485 National Park Drive
Twenty-nine Palms, CA 92277-3597
(619) 367-7511

Lassen National Park
Superintendent's Office
55 South Sacramento Street
Susanville, CA 96130
(916) 257-2451

Lassen Volcanic National Park
Highway 36, east of Red Bluff
Superintendent's Office
P.O. Box 100
Mineral, CA 96063-0100
(916) 595-4444

Redwood National Park
Off Highway 101
Superintendent's Office
1111 Second Street
Crescent City, CA 95531
(707) 464-6101

**Sequoia and Kings Canyon
National Park**
Highway 180, east of Highway 99
Superintendent's Office
Three Rivers, CA 93271
(209) 565-3134

Yosemite National Park
Park Superintendent's Office
P.O. Box 577
Yosemite National Park, CA 95389
(209) 372-0200 or 372-0265

❖ NATIONAL RECREATION AREAS

Golden Gate National Recreation Area
General Superintendent's Office
Building 201 – Fort Mason
San Francisco, CA 94123
(415) 556-0560

Santa Monica Mountains National Recreation Area
Superintendent's Office
30401 Agoura Road, Suite 100
Agoura Hills, CA 91301
(818) 597-9192, ext. 201, or
    800-533-7275

Whiskeytown-Shasta-Trinity National Recreation Area
Off of S.R. 299 near Whiskeytown, 8 miles
    west of Redding
(916) 246-1225

❖ NATIONAL FOREST GENERAL INFORMATION

Pacific-Southwest Region
U.S. Forest Service
630 Sasome Street, Room 527
San Francisco, CA 94111
(415) 705-2874
800-280-CAMP (for information and
    camping reservations)

❖ NATIONAL FORESTS

Angeles National Forest
Highways 2 and 39
Supervisor's Office
701 N. Santa Anita Avenue
Arcadia, CA 91006
(818) 574-5200

Cleveland National Forest
Supervisor's Office
10845 Rancho Bernardo Road, Suite 200
San Diego, CA 92127
(619) 674-2901 or 673-6180

Eldorado National Forest
Eldorado County
Highway 50, east of Highway 49
Visitors Center
3070 Camino Heights Drive
Camino, CA 95709
(916) 644-6048

Inyo National Forest
Supervisor's Office
873 North Main Street
Bishop, CA 93514
(619) 873-2400
Hours and information call:
(619) 876-4252

Klamath National Forest
Forest Supervisor's Office
1312 Fairlane Road
Yreka, CA 96097
(916) 842-6131

Lassen National Forest
Supervisor's Office
55 South Sacramento Street
Susanville, CA 96130
(916) 257-2151

Los Padres National Forest
Forest Supervisor's Office
6144 Calle Real
Goleta, CA 93117
(805) 683-6711

Mendocino National Forest
Glenn County
Off Highway 162, east of Highway 101
Forest Supervisor's Office
420 East Laurel Street
Willows, CA 95988
(916) 934-2350
or
Mendocino National Forest
Mendocino County
Covelo Ranger District
Covelo
(707) 983-6118

Modoc National Forest
Forest Supervisor's Office
800 West 12th Street
Alturas, CA 96101
(916) 233-5811

Plumas National Forest
Ranger Station and Forest Headquarters
Box 11500
Quincy, CA 95971
(916) 283-2050

San Bernardino National Forest
Highway 18
Forest Supervisor's Office
1824 South Commercenter Circle
San Bernardino, CA 92408-3430
(909) 383-5588

Sequoia National Forest
Highway 180, along Highway 190
Forest Supervisor's Office
900 West Grand Avenue
Porterville, CA 93257-2035
(209) 297-0706 or 784-1500

Shasta-Trinity National Forest
Forest Supervisor's Office
2400 Washington Avenue
Redding, CA 96001
(916) 246-5222

Sierra National Forest
Highway 41 and Highway 168
Forest Headquarters
1600 Tollhouse Road
Clovis, CA 93611
(209) 297-0706

Six Rivers National Forest
Forest Supervisor's Office
1330 Bayshore Way
Eureka, CA 95001
(707) 441-3523 or 442-1721

Stanislaus National Forest
Highways 4, 108 and 120
Tuolumne County
Supervisor's Office
19777 Greenley Road
Sonora, CA 95370
(209) 532-3671

Tahoe National Forest
Interstate 80 and Highways 20, 49, 89 and
   267
Forest Supervisor's Office
631 Coyote Street
P.O. Box 6003
Nevada City, CA 95959
(916) 265-4531

NATIONAL PRESERVES, RESERVES AND SEASHORES

Mojave National Preserve
Between Interstate 40 and Interstate 15
Preserve Office
222 East Main Street
Barstow, CA 92311
(619) 255-8760 or 255-8801

Tule Elk State Reserve
Station and Morris roads, off Stockdale
   Highway
Bakersfield, CA
(805) 765-5004

Point Reyes National Seashore
West of Highway 1, between Bolinas and
 Inverness
Superintendent's Office
Point Reyes National Seashore
Point Reyes, CA 94956
(415) 663-1092

STATE PARK
GENERAL INFORMATION

California State Park System
Department of Parks and Recreation
P.O. Box 942896
Sacramento, CA 94296-0001
(916) 653-6995

STATE PARKS AND
RECREATION AREAS

Anderson Marsh State Park
Highway 53
Lower Lake and Clear Lake
(707) 994-0688 or 279-2267

Andrew Molera State Park
Off Highway 1
Big Sur
(408) 667-2315

Annadel State Park
Channel Drive, off Montgomery Drive
Santa Rosa
(707) 539-3911 or 938-1519

Anza-Borrego Desert State Park
West Palm Canyon Drive
Borrego Springs
(619) 767-4684 or 767-5311

Armstrong Redwoods State Park
Armstrong Woods Road, off Highway 116
Guerneville
(707) 869-2015 or 865-2391

Auburn State Recreation Area
Highway 49, one mile south of Highway 80
Auburn
(916) 885-4527

Austin Creek State Recreation Area
Armstrong Woods Road, near Sweetwater
 Springs Road
Guerneville
(707) 869-2015 or 865-2391

Bethany Reservoir State Park
South of Byron on Christensen Road
Northeast of Livermore in Waterford
(209) 874-2056

Big Basin Redwoods State Park
Northwest of Boulder Creek on Highway 236
Big Basin
(408) 338-6132 or 338-8860

Bodie State Historic Park
Southeast of Bridgeport via U.S. 395 and
 S.R. 270
Bodie
(619) 647-6445

Bothe-Napa Valley State Park
Highway 29
St. Helena
(707) 942-4575

Brannan Island State Park
Highway 160, 13 miles north of Antioch
 Bridge
Sacramento County
(916) 777-6671

Calaveras Big Trees State Park
Highway 4
Arnold
(209) 795-2334

Castaic Lake State Recreation Area
Ridge Route and Lake Hughes Roads
Senca Hills
(805) 257-4050

Castle Crags State Park
Off Interstate 5
Dunsmuir
(916) 235-2684

Caswell Memorial State Park
South Austin Road
Stanislaus County
(209) 599-3810

Clear Lake State Park
5300 Soda Bay Road
Kelseyville, CA 95451
(707) 279-4293

Columbia State Park
Sierra Nevada foothills
Columbia
(209) 532-4644

Colusa-Sacramento River State Recreation Area
Highway 20, 9 miles east of Interstate 5
Colusa
(916) 458-4927

Cuyamaca Rancho State Park
Highway 79, between Highway 78 and
    Interstate 8
San Diego County
(619) 765-0755

Del Norte Coast Redwoods State Park
Cresent City
(707) 464-9533

D.L. Bliss State Park
Highway 89, 8 miles south of Tahoma
South Lake Tahoe
(916) 525-7277 or 525-7232

Empire Mine State Historic Park
10791 East Empire Street
Grass Valley, CA 95945
(916) 273-8522

Fremont Peak State Park
Highway 156 on San Juan Canyon Road
San Juan Bautista
(408) 623-4255

Garland Ranch Regional Park
700 W. Carmel Valley Road
Carmel Valley, CA 93924
(408) 659-4488

Grizzly Creek Redwoods State Park
Highway 36, 17 miles east of Highway 101
Birdgeville
(707) 777-3683

Henry Cowell Redwoods State Park
Highway 9
Felton
(408) 335-4598

Humboldt Lagoons State Park
Off U.S. 101
Orick
(707) 488-2041

Jack London State Historic Park
London Ranch Road, off Arnold Drive
Glen Ellen
(707) 938-5216

Jedediah Smith Redwoods State Park
Off Highway 101
Cresent City
(707) 458-3310

Lake Elsinore State Recreation Area
Highway 74, 3 miles west of Interstate 15 at
    Central Avenue exit
Lake Elsinore
(909) 674-3177

Lake Perris State Recreation Area
Lake Perris Drive, off Ramona Expressway
Perris
(909) 657-0676

Mac Kerricher State Park
Mac Kerricher Road, off Highway 1
Cleone, near Fort Bragg
(707) 937-5804

Manchester Beach State Park
Kinney Road, near Highway 1
Point Arena
(707) 937-5804

**McArthur-Burney Falls Memorial
State Park**
Highway 89 and Pacific Crest National
    Scenic Trail
Burney
(916) 335-2777

Millerton Lake State Recreation Area
5290 Millerton Road
Friant
(209) 822-2332

Mount Diablo State Park
Mount Diablo Scenic Boulevard
East of Danville
(510) 837-2525

Palomar Mountain State Park
Route S-6
Palomar Valley
(619) 742-3462

Patrick's Point State Park
Highway 255
Manila – Humboldt Bay
(Dogs are restricted from the beach and
    trails.)
(707) 677-3570

Plumas-Eureka State Park
County Road A14, west of Highway 89
310 Johnsville Road
Johnsville, CA 96103
(916) 836-2380

Point Mugu State Park
Las Posas Road
Ventura County
(805) 488-5223

Prairie Creek Redwoods State Park
Off Highway 101
Orick
(707) 488-2171

Pyramid Lake State Park
S.R. 445, off Highway 395
Sutcliffe
(702) 476-1155

Richardson Grove State Park
Highway 101
Gaberville
(707) 247-3318

South Yuba River Project State Park
Pleasant Valley Road, 8 miles north of
    Highway 20
Penn Valley
(916) 432-2546 or 273-3884

OTHER
RECREATIONAL
AREAS

**Anthony Chabot Regional Park and
Lake Chabot Marina**
Redwood Road
Castro Valley
(510) 635-0138 x2571

Contra Loma Regional Park
Frederickson Lane, west of Empire Mine
    Road
Antioch
(510) 635-0135

Cow Mountain Recreation Area
Mill Creek Road, off Highway 101
Ukiah
(707) 468-4000

Del Valle Regional Park
Del Valle Road, south of Mines Road
South of Livermore
(510) 373-0332

Don Pedro Lake
Bonds Flat Road, off La Grange Road
Stanislaus County
(209) 852-2396

Doran and Westside Regional Parks
Doran Park Road, off Highway 1
Bodega Bay
(707) 875-3540

Eagle Lake
Off Eagle Lake Road
Susanville
(916) 257-2151 or Ranger District, 257-4188

Gualala Point Regional Park
Highway 1
Gualala
(707) 785-2377

Lake Arrowhead
Communities Chamber of Commerce
28200 Highway 189, Building "J"
PO Box 219
Lake Arrowhead, CA 92352
(909) 336-6992

Lake Berryessa
Berryessa Knoxville Road off Highway 128
Yolo County, Napa
(707) 966-1419

Lake Casitas Recreation Area
Santa Ana Road and Highway 150
Ventura County
(805) 649-2233

Lake Sonoma
Visitors Center
3333 Skaggs Springs Road
Geyerville, CA 95441
(707) 433-9483

Lake Nacimiento
Off Highway 101
Between King City and Paso Robles, Jolon
    exit
Monterey County
800-323-3839

Martinez Regional Shoreline
North Court Street, north of Ferry Street
Martinez
(510) 635-0135

Mission Bay Park
2688 East Mission Drive
San Diego
(619) 221-8900 or 276-8200

Spring Lake Regional Park
Newanga Avenue, off Summerfield Road
Santa Rosa
(707) 539-8092

Sunol – Ohlone Regional Wilderness
Geary Road, off Calaveras Road
Sunol
(510) 862-2244

**Vasona Park and Reservoir/Oak
Meadow Park**
University Avenue and Garden Hill Drive, off
    Blossom Hill Road
Los Gatos
(408) 358-3751 or 356-2729 – Vasona Park
(408) 354-6809 – Oak Meadow Park

Kennel Information For Major California Attractions

DISNEYLAND
1313 Harbor Boulevard
Anaheim, CA 92803
(714) 781-4560 or 999-4565
Kennels are on site.
Fee: $10 per day

KNOTT'S BERRY FARM
8039 Beach Boulevard
Buena Park, CA 90620
(714) 827-1776
No kennels on site. Call for a list of nearby
kennels.

MARINE WORLD AFRICA USA
Located at Marine World Parkway, S.R. 37
exit, off Interstate 80.
Vallejo, CA 95489
(707) 644-4000 or 643-6722
No kennels on site. Call for a list of nearby
kennels.

PARAMOUNT'S GREAT AMERICA
Located on Great America Parkway between
U.S. 101 and S.R. 237.
Santa Clara, CA 95054
(408) 988-1776
No kennels on site. Call for a list of nearby
kennels.

SAN DIEGO WILD ANIMAL PARK
via Rancho Parkway off Interstate 15
Escondido, CA 92026
(619) 234-6541
No kennels on site. Call for a list of nearby
kennels.

SAN DIEGO ZOO
P.O. Box 551
San Diego, CA 92112
(619) 234-3153
No kennels on site. Call for a list of nearby
kennels.

SEA WORLD
1720 South Shores Road
San Diego, CA 92109
(619) 222-6363
Kennels are on site.
Fee: $5 per day

SIX FLAGS MAGIC MOUNTAIN
P.O. Box 5500
Located off Highway 5
Valencia, CA 91355
(805) 255-4100
Kennels are on site.
Fee: No charge to park visitors

UNIVERSAL STUDIO HOLLYWOOD
Lankershim Boulevard Freeway – U.S. 101
Universal City, CA 91608
(818) 508-9600
Kennels are on site.
Fee: No charge to park visitors. Stop by
Visitor's Services.

Index

About the Author...from a dog's point of view

Dreamer Dawg, office manager and "cover girl" for Bon Vivant Press, is a nine-year-young Labrador Retriever. When not exploring the food and lodging for each regional book, you can find Dreamer relaxing onboard her boat in the Monterey harbor or running with the horses in the Salinas Valley.

Owners Robert & Kathleen Fish, authors of the popular "Secrets" series, have researched and written fifteen award-winning cookbooks and travel books, and are always on the lookout for lodgings with style and character.

Other titles in the Pets Welcome™ series are *Pets Welcome™ America's South*, *Pets Welcome™ Pacific Northwest*, *Pets Welcome™ New England* and *Pets Welcome™ Florida*.

Bon Vivant Press

A division of The Millennium Publishing Group

PO Box 1994

Monterey, CA 93942

800-524-6826 • 408-373-0592 • 408-373-3567 FAX • Website: http://www.millpub.com

Send _____ copies of **Pets Welcome California** at $15.95 each.

Send _____ copies of **Pets Welcome America's South** at $15.95 each.

Send _____ copies of **Cooking With the Masters of Food & Wine** at $34.95 each.

Send _____ copies of **The Elegant Martini** at $17.95 each.

Send _____ copies of **Cooking Secrets From Around the World** at $15.95 each.

Send _____ copies of **Cooking Secrets From America's South** at $15.95 each.

Send _____ copies of **Louisiana Cooking Secrets** at $15.95 each.

Send _____ copies of **Pacific Northwest Cooking Secrets** at $15.95 each.

Send _____ copies of **Cooking Secrets for Healthy Living** at $15.95 each.

Send _____ copies of **The Great California Cookbook** at $14.95 each.

Send _____ copies of **The Gardener's Cookbook** at $15.95 each.

Send _____ copies of **The Great Vegetarian Cookbook** at $15.95 each.

Send _____ copies of **California Wine Country Cooking Secrets** at $14.95 each.

Send _____ copies of **San Francisco's Cooking Secrets** at $13.95 each.

Send _____ copies of **Monterey's Cooking Secrets** at $13.95 each.

Send _____ copies of **New England's Cooking Secrets** at $14.95 each.

Send _____ copies of **Cape Cod's Cooking Secrets** at $14.95 each.

Send _____ copies of **Jewish Cooking Secrets From Here and Far** at $14.95 each.

Add $3.00 postage and handling for the first book ordered and $1.50 for each additional book. Please add $1.08 sales tax per book, for those books shipped to California addresses.

Please charge my ☐ Visa   # _____
☐ MasterCard

Expiration date _____ Signature _____

Enclosed is my check for _____

Name _____

Address _____

City _____ State _____ ZIP _____

☐ **This is a gift. Send directly to:**

Name _____

Address _____

City _____ State _____ ZIP _____

☐ **Autographed by the author**

Autographed to _____

Reader's Response Card

Please return to:
Bon Vivant Press
P.O. Box 1994
Monterey, CA 93942
Fax your information to: (408) 373-3567

Please assist us in updating our next edition. If you have discovered an interesting or charming inn, hotel, guest ranch or spa in California that allows pets, or any special neighborhood parks in California that allow pets, with or without a leash, please let us hear from you and include the following information:

Type of lodging (check one):
☐ Bed and Breakfast   ☐ Hotel   ☐ Inn   ☐ Guest Ranch   ☐ Spa

Lodging Address _____

City _____ State _____ ZIP _____

Phone (_____) _____

Comments _____

_____

_____

Park Name _____

Address or Cross Streets _____

City _____ State _____ ZIP _____

Phone: (if known) (_____) _____ Leashes required? Yes | No

Comments _____

_____

We appreciate your assistance. It is wonderful to discover new and interesting places to take your pets. If you have made a discovery of your own—a unique or charming inn, hotel, guest ranch or spa that allows pets, or perhaps a special neighborhood park, beach, or recreational area—please share your discovery with us, so that we might include it in future editions.

Notes